THE REVELS PLAYS

THE LOVER'S MELANCHOLY

JOHN FORD

Edited by

R. F. Hill

MANCHESTER
UNIVERSITY PRESS

© R. F. Hill 1985

All rights reserved

Published by Manchester University Press
Oxford Road, Manchester M13 9PL
and 51 Washington Street, Dover,
New Hampshire 03820, USA

ISBN 0 7190 1533 2 *cased*

British Library Cataloguing in Publication Data

Ford, John, *b. ca 1586*
　　The lover's melancholy.—(The Revels plays)
　　I. Title　II. Hill, R. F.　III. Series
　　822'.3　　PR2524.L6

Library of Congress Cataloging in Publication Data

Ford, John, 1586–ca. 1640.
　　The lover's melancholy.
　　(The Revels plays)
　　Includes index.
　　I. Hill, R. F.　II. Title.　III. Series.
PR2524.L6 1985　　822'.3　　84-12263

Typeset by August Filmsetting, Haydock, St Helens
Printed in Great Britain by Bell and Bain Ltd., Glasgow

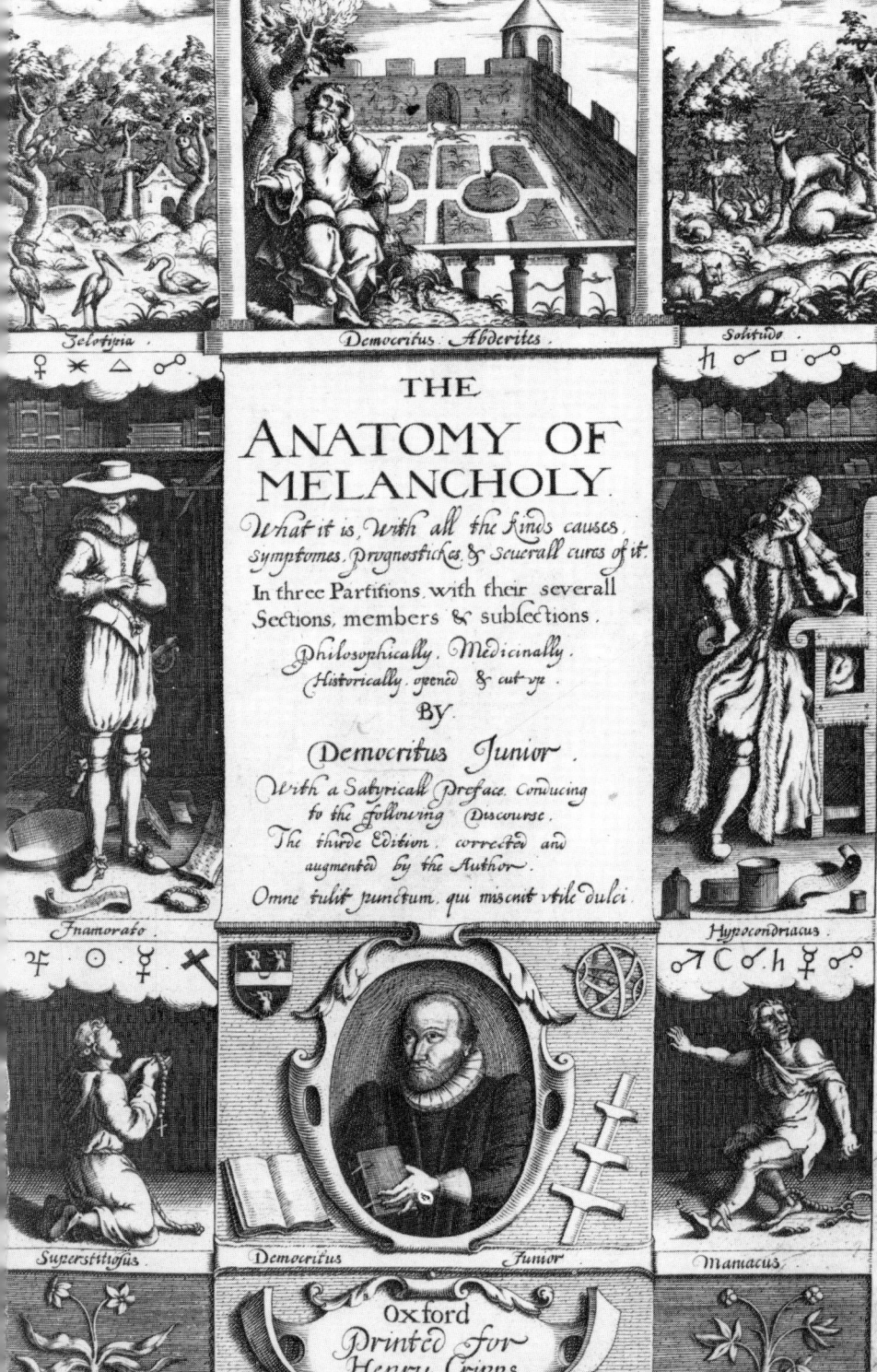

THE REVELS PLAYS

ANON. *Arden of Faversham   The Second Maiden's Tragedy*
Two Tudor Interludes: *Youth* and *Hick Scorner*

BEAUMONT *The Knight of the Burning Pestle*
A Yorkshire Tragedy
——AND FLETCHER *Philaster*★

CHAPMAN *Bussy d'Ambois*★
——JOHNSON AND MARSTON *Eastward Ho*

DEKKER *The Shoemaker's Holiday*

FARQUHAR *The Recruiting Officer*

FORD *The Broken Heart   'Tis Pity she's a Whore*
The Lover's Melancholy

GREENE *James the Fourth*★

JONSON *The Alchemist*★ *Bartholomew Fair*★
Volpone   The New Inn

KYD *The Spanish Tragedy*

MARLOWE *Doctor Faustus*★ *The Jew of Malta*★
The Poems   Tamburlaine I and II

MARSTON *Antonio's Revenge   The Fawn   The Malcontent*
——AND OTHERS *The Insatiate Countess*

MIDDLETON *Women Beware Women*★
——AND ROWLEY *The Changeling*★

PEELE *The Old Wives Tale*

SKELTON *Magnificence*

TOURNEUR *The Revenger's Tragedy*★

VANBRUGH *The Provoked Wife*

WEBSTER *The Duchess of Malfi*★ *The White Devil*★

WYCHERLEY *The Country Wife*

★ available in paperback

THE REVELS PLAYS

Founder Editor
Clifford Leech 1958–71

General Editors
F. David Hoeniger, E. A. J. Honigmann and J. R. Mulryne

THE LOVER'S MELANCHOLY

Frontispiece: Title page of Robert Burton's *The Anatomy of Melancholy*; engraved by Christian Le Blon and first printed in the third edition, 1628

Contents

LIST OF ILLUSTRATIONS	vi
GENERAL EDITORS' PREFACE	vii
PREFACE	ix
ABBREVIATIONS	x
INTRODUCTION	
1 Date	1
2 Sources	3
3 Dramaturgy	10
4 Therapy	19
5 Values	21
6 Style	25
7 The play and Ford's earlier works	28
8 Tragicomedy	30
9 Stage History	32
10 Text	33
The Lover's Melancholy	43
APPENDICES	
A Source of the 'musical duel' (I.i.106–70): Famiamus Strada, *Prolusiones Academicae, Oratoriae, Historicae, Poeticae*	152
B Musical setting of 'Fly hence, shadows, that do keep' (V.ii.1–10): John Wilson, *Cheerful Ayres or Ballads*	154
GLOSSARIAL INDEX TO THE COMMENTARY	157

Illustrations

Frontispiece: Title page of Robert Burton's *The Anatomy of Melancholy*; engraved by Christian Le Blon and first printed in the third edition, 1628

Page xii Title page of the 1629 Quarto of *The Lover's Melancholy*

Both are reproduced by permission of the British Library.

General Editors' Preface

The series known as the Revels Plays was conceived by Clifford Leech. The idea for the series emerged in his mind, as he explained in his preface to the first of the Revels Plays in 1958, from the success of the New Arden Shakespeare. The aim of the new group of texts was 'to apply to Shakespeare's predecessors, contemporaries and successors the methods that are now used in Shakespeare editing'. The plays chosen were to include well known works from the early Tudor period to about 1700, as well as others less familiar but of literary and theatrical merit: 'the plays included,' Leech wrote, 'should be such as to deserve and indeed demand performance.' We owe it to Clifford Leech that the idea became reality. He set the high standards of the series, ensuring that editors of individual volumes produced work of lasting merit, equally useful for teachers and students, theatre directors and actors. Clifford Leech remained General Editor until 1971, supervising the first seventeen volumes to be published.

The Revels Plays are now under the direction of three General Editors, F. David Hoeniger, E. A. J. Honigmann and J. R. Mulryne. The publishers, originally Methuen, are now Manchester University Press. Despite these changes, the format and essential character of the series will continue, and it is hoped that its editorial standards will be maintained. Except for some work in progress, the General Editors intend, in expanding the series, to concentrate for the immediate future on plays from the period 1558–1642, and may include a small number of non-dramatic works of interest to students of drama. Some slight changes have been forced by considerations of cost. For example, in editions from 1978, notes to the introduction are placed together at the end, not at the foot of the page. Collation and commentary notes will continue, however, to appear on the relevant pages.

The text of each Revels play, in accordance with established practice in the series, is edited afresh from the original text of best authority (in a few instances, texts), but spelling and punctuation are modernised and speech headings are silently made consistent. Elisions in the original are also silently regularised, except where metre would be affected by the change; since 1968 the '-ed' form is used for non-syllabic terminations in past tenses and past participles ('-'d' earlier), and '-èd' for syllabic ('-ed' earlier). The editor emends, as distinct from modernises, his original only in instances where error is patent, or at least very probable, and correction persuasive. Act divisions are given only if they appear in the original or if the structure of the play clearly points to them. Those act and scene divisions not found in the original are provided unobtrusively in small type and in square brackets. Square brackets are also used for any other additions to or changes in the stage directions of the original.

Revels Plays do not provide a variorum collation, but only those variants which require the critical attention of serious textual students. All departures of substance from 'copy-text' are listed, including any relineation and those changes in punctuation which involve to any degree a decision between alternative interpretations; but not such accidentals as turned letters, nor necessarily additions to stage directions whose editorial nature is already made clear by the use of brackets. Press corrections in the 'copy-text' are likewise included. Of later emendations of the text, only those are given which as alternative readings still deserve attention.

One of the hallmarks of the Revels Plays is the thoroughness of their annotations. Besides explaining the meaning of difficult words and passages, the editor provides comments on customs or usage, text or stage-business—indeed, on anything he judges pertinent and helpful. Each volume contains a Glossarial Index to the Commentary, in which particular attention is drawn to meanings for words not listed in *O.E.D.*

The Introduction to a Revels play assesses the authority of the 'copy-text' on which it is based, and discusses the editorial methods employed in dealing with it; the editor also considers his play's date and (where relevant) sources, together with its place in the work of the author and in the theatre of its time. Stage history is offered, and in the case of a play by an author not previously represented in the series a brief biography is given.

It is our hope that plays edited in this fashion will promote further scholarly and theatrical investigation of one of the richest periods in theatrical history.

F. DAVID HOENIGER
E. A. J. HONIGMANN
J. R. MULRYNE

Preface

This edition was first read in an early draft by Professor F. D. Hoeniger and to him I am grateful for encouragement and for general advice on the Introduction. Above all I am indebted to Professor E. A. J. Honigmann for the correction of detail and the many other improvements which resulted from his careful reading of the typescript. My thanks are also due to my colleague, Richard Proudfoot, for valuable guidance on textual matters, and to another colleague, Mrs Olga Illston, for tidying up points in my translation of Strada's 'Musical Duel'. The edition has benefited from all such advice, but as the final decisions have been mine responsibility for deficiencies rests with me. What I owe to previous Ford scholars is everywhere apparent. I wish to record my thanks to Mr Lewis Jones for his editorial work on the song setting of Appendix B; also to the Provost and Fellows of Eton College for granting me permission to collate their copy of the Quarto, and to libraries and colleges in Scotland and the U.S.A. listed on p. 34 for providing photocopies. A final word of especial thanks must go to my colleagues for their generosity in lightening my responsibilities in the department during the last stages of work on this edition.

King's College, London   R.F.H.

Abbreviations

EDITIONS COLLATED

Q	The Quarto of 1629. For copies of Q collated see Introduction, p. 34.
Weber	*The Dramatic Works of John Ford*, ed. Henry Weber 2 vols. (Edinburgh, 1811), vol. I.
Gifford	*The Dramatic Works of John Ford*, ed. William Gifford 2 vols. (London, 1827), vol. I.
Dyce	*The Works of John Ford ... by William Gifford, Esq. A New Edition, Carefully Revised ... by the Rev. Alexander Dyce* 3 vols. (London, 1869), vol. I.
Ellis	*The Best Plays of ... John Ford*, ed. Havelock Ellis (London, 1888, Mermaid Series).

OTHER WORKS

Abbott	E. A. Abbott, *A Shakespearian Grammar* (London, 1869; ed. cit., 1901).
Anderson	Donald K. Anderson Jr., *John Ford* (New York, 1972).
Babb	Lawrence Babb, *The Elizabethan Malady: A Study of Melancholia in English Literature from 1580 to 1642* (East Lansing, 1951).
Bentley	Gerald Eades Bentley, *The Jacobean and Caroline Stage* (7 vols., Oxford, 1941–68).
Burton	Robert Burton, *The Anatomy of Melancholy*, edd. Floyd Dell and Paul Jordan-Smith (2 vols., New York, 1927; ed. cit., 1938). Page references to this edition are followed by references to Burton's division into Partition, Section, Member, Sub-section, cited simply as four numerals; citations of three numerals refer to Partition, Section, Member.
Davril	Robert Davril, *Le Drame de John Ford* (Paris, 1954).
Ewing	S. Blaine Ewing, *Burtonian Melancholy in the Plays of John Ford* (Princeton, 1940).
Leech	Clifford Leech, *John Ford and the Drama of his Time* (London and Toronto, 1957).
Linthicum	M. C. Linthicum, *Costume in the Drama of Shakespeare and his Contemporaries* (Oxford, 1936).
L.M.	*The Lover's Melancholy.*
Oliver	H. J. Oliver, *The Problem of John Ford* (Melbourne, London and New York, 1955).
O.E.D.	*The Oxford English Dictionary.*
Partridge	Eric Partridge, *Shakespeare's Bawdy* (London, 1947; ed. cit., 1968).

ABBREVIATIONS

Revels History	*The Revels History of Drama in English: Volume III 1576–1613*, General Editors Clifford Leech and T. W. Craik (London, 1975).
Sargeant	M. Joan Sargeant, *John Ford* (Oxford, 1935).
Sensabaugh	G. F. Sensabaugh, *The Tragic Muse of John Ford* (Stanford, California, and London, 1944).
Stavig	Mark Stavig, *John Ford and the Traditional Moral Order* (Madison, Milwaukee and London, 1968).
Tilley	Morris Palmer Tilley, *A Dictionary of the Proverbs in England in the Sixteenth and Seventeenth Centuries* (Ann Arbor, Michigan, 1950).

Ford's other works are normally cited from the three-volume edition by Dyce, and Beaumont and Fletcher's plays from *The Works of Francis Beaumont and John Fletcher*, edd. Arnold Glover and A. R. Waller (10 vols., Cambridge, 1905–12); neither of these editions gives line numbers so references are to act and scene, followed by volume and page. For Shakespeare, Jonson and Massinger the following editions are cited: *William Shakespeare: The Complete Works*, ed. Peter Alexander (London and Glasgow, 1951); *Ben Jonson*, edd. C. H. Herford and Percy and Evelyn Simpson (11 vols., Oxford, 1925–52); *The Plays and Poems of Philip Massinger*, edd. Philip Edwards and Colin Gibson (5 vols., Oxford, 1976).

THE
LOVERS
Melancholy.

Acted
**AT THE PRIVATE
HOVSE IN THE BLACKE**
Friers, and publikely at the Globe
by the Kings Maiesties Ser-
uants.

LONDON,
Printed for *H. Seile*, and are to be sold at the Ty-
gers head in Saint *Pauls* Church-yard.
1 6 2 9.

Title page of the 1629 Quarto of *The Lover's Melancholy*

Introduction

1. DATE

Ford's dramatic career began with a period of collaborative writing (1621–5) and *The Lover's Melancholy* was his first play of independent authorship to be published (1629).[1] It was licensed for stage performance on 24 November 1628 and it is a reasonable assumption that it was written not long before. With the exception of *The Lady's Trial*, licensed 3 May 1638, the order of composition of Ford's other independent plays is a matter of conjecture. Their dates of publication are: *The Broken Heart*, *'Tis Pity She's a Whore*, *Love's Sacrifice*, 1633; *Perkin Warbeck*, 1634; *The Fancies Chaste and Noble*, 1638; *The Queen*, 1653 (published anonymously but now generally accepted as the work of Ford). The point for consideration here is whether any of these plays preceded *The Lover's Melancholy* in composition. Sargeant and Davril agree in placing *'Tis Pity* and *Love's Sacrifice* a little before it,[2] while Bentley is at least prepared to entertain the view that *The Broken Heart* may have been written as early as 1627, being especially disturbed, as others have been, by the notion that because *The Lover's Melancholy* is inferior to Ford's tragedies it must have been written before them.[3] Roper, after a careful weighing of such flimsy evidence as exists for dating *'Tis Pity*, is unable to date the play more precisely than as having been written between 1615 and 1633 although he inclines towards the early part of that period, agreeing with Leech as to the play's Jacobean character.[4] He tentatively advances the theory that *'Tis Pity*, *Love's Sacrifice* and *Perkin Warbeck*, all performed at the Phoenix theatre and therefore often grouped with Ford's two other Phoenix plays, *The Lady's Trial* and *The Fancies*, may belong to an earlier period of writing for the Phoenix before the Blackfriars plays, *The Lover's Melancholy* and *The Broken Heart*. Ford had already written in collaboration for the Phoenix during the years 1621–4.[5] Roper bases his conjecture on what might be possible given the companies and theatres for which Ford wrote, but there are other considerations.

'Tis Pity and *Love's Sacrifice* were published in 1633, and *Perkin Warbeck* in 1634; we do not know when they were first performed, and considerable time might intervene between such performance and publication. However, two of Ford's plays were published in the year following first performance; *The Lover's Melancholy*, licensed

24 November 1628, published 1629; *The Lady's Trial*, licensed 3 May 1638, published 1639. This proves nothing about his other plays but it shows that in two instances he was quick to go into print where there was presumably no objection from the acting companies concerned. It is to be noted that in his dedication to *The Lover's Melancholy* Ford shows a snobbish queasiness about his first venture in having a play printed. Having mastered his scruples he might have been the readier to go into print quickly with his other plays if circumstances allowed.

In discussing the date of *'Tis Pity* Roper points out that there is no specific debt to Burton's *Anatomy of Melancholy* (1621) and that Ford could have been drawing on earlier books such as Bright's *Treatise of Melancholie* (1586, repr. 1613) or on received ideas.[6] While this may be true most critics of Ford accept that Burton's popular treatise was of importance in determining in a general way his interest in morbid psychology, particularly in respect of sexual love. It seems rather unusual that if Ford wrote some of his major plays before 1628 he should only then acknowledge a debt to Burton in a marginal note to *The Lover's Melancholy*[7] and, moreover, use *The Anatomy* in a more obvious and mechanical way than he had done hitherto. The overt dependence of that play on *The Anatomy* suggests an early exploration of its possibilities, but one which is in some ways too close to the work to produce an entirely satisfactory result.

The view that *The Lover's Melancholy* was Ford's first independent play may gain some support from commendatory verses to the play written by William Singleton who had joined Ford at the Middle Temple in 1626. He first pays tribute to what Ford has already achieved as a writer:

> Nor seek I fame for thee, when thine own pen
> Hath forced a praise long since from knowing men.

'Long since' suggests a reference to Ford's non-dramatic works published between 1606 and 1620, but of course it is an inexact phrase and could refer to dramatic works of a more recent date. The succeeding lines are optative:

> I speak my thoughts and *wish* unto the stage
> A glory from thy studies, that the age
> *May be* indebted to thee for reprieve
> Of purer language, and that spite *may* grieve
> To see itself outdone. When thou art read

The theatre *may* hope arts are not dead,
Though long concealed. (Italics mine)

Here the thought is for what Ford may achieve in the theatre, which could be understood as heralding a new dramatist on the scene, and Singleton might not have written in this vein had several of Ford's plays already been in existence. Arguably the last three lines could refer merely to publication but to interpret 'long concealed' as unpublished is disputable given the coterie nature of the literary and theatrical world of the day, and the fact that works were often circulated in manuscript.

My reading of Singleton's lines is supported by the commendatory verses of Humfrey Howarth who joined Ford at the Middle Temple in 1624. He dwells upon Ford's doubts about the worth of his play and concludes:

Established fame will thy physician be,
Write but again to cure thy jealousy.

Would Howarth have written thus about a dramatist whose major plays had already established him in the theatre? Clearly, the evidential value of commendatory verses is not great where the mode of expression is imprecise, but at least these men were close friends of Ford. It should also be added that the commendatory verses to his other plays give no comparable suggestion of an emerging dramatist. My arguments for the view that *The Lover's Melancholy* was the first of Ford's plays of independent authorship to be written[8] are not confidently advanced but where evidence for chronology is so meagre any additional scraps may be welcome.

2. SOURCES

Ford tells us in the Prologue that the play is all of his own devising except for a few 'stolen invention(s)' which any scholar would regard as legitimate. He might have made the same remark about his other plays for, with the exception of *Perkin Warbeck*, it would appear that he himself created the stories of his plays. There is, however, considerable echoing of situations and types from earlier plays and this is very evident in *The Lover's Melancholy*. In addition, two important sources are acknowledged in marginal notes.

The play is set in Cyprus, appropriately enough since legend has it that Venus, after her birth from the sea, landed at Paphos in Cyprus and the worship of Venus became prevalent there. However, Ford makes nothing specific of that association despite the play's love concerns and there is only one mention of Venus (III.ii.60). References at II.i.67–74 concerning the detainment of Cretan ships and a Syrian claim to tribute from Cyprus, together with Sophronos' speech (II.i.1–16) on its insecure state, suggest Ford's general acquaintance with its chequered fortunes as a pawn in the power struggle in the eastern Mediterranean. In early times Cyprus was successively under tribute to Assyrian, Egyptian, Persian and Roman empires[9] but a scanning of likely classical authorities has revealed nothing conclusive as regards Ford's possible reading. He could have learned from the Greek historian Diodorus Siculus about the fortunes of Cyprus during its tributary relation to Persia in the fifth and fourth centuries B.C., and his attention might well have been drawn to this period by Isocrates'[10] panegyric on Evagoras, king of Salamis (c. 411–374), a city in Cyprus, and his oration on kingly duties to Nicocles, son of Evagoras. If Ford conceived of a particular time in the history of Cyprus for his play this would have been eminently suitable. Both orations of Isocrates stress the strong affiliations with Greece during the reign of Evagoras, and it was certainly the period of the flourishing of 'schools of sacred knowledge' to which Ford refers (V.ii.178). Of course, the court of Ford's Cyprus is Jacobean in manners but it is nonetheless true that the lofty moral tone in which Isocrates writes of the reign of Evagoras would be appropriate to the court of Palador.

A marginal note to I.i.106–9 refers to Book II, Exercise VI of the *Prolusiones Academicae, Oratoriae, Historicae, Poeticae* (1617) of the Jesuit Famiamus Strada which contains the episode of a musical duel between a lutanist and a nightingale, written in imitation of the Latin poetry of Claudian. The *Prolusiones* were reprinted in 1619, 1625, 1631, and the musical duel was frequently imitated in the seventeenth century, notably by Crashaw.[11] Crashaw was sixteen or seventeen when *The Lover's Melancholy* was published; his 'Musicks Duel' was first printed in *The Delights of the Muses* (1646) and although it is contained in a manuscript anthology which Martin thinks cannot be later than 1634,[12] there is little likelihood that Ford knew Crashaw's poem even if we assume it to have been written as early as 1628. Certainly there is no kinship between Ford's narration of the duel and Crashaw's elaborately conceited and much expanded version of Strada; either they derive independently from Strada or Ford's suggested Crashaw's version.

INTRODUCTION

Strada's poem (translation) is given in Appendix A and it will be seen that Ford follows it in general outline but prunes the verbosity. However, the two are markedly different since one is an independent poem and the other part of the fabric of a play. In Ford's play it is Menaphon's narration of his first encounter with Parthenophill, the lutanist, and the responses of the narrator are as important as the story itself for our introduction to Parthenophill. The music entranced Menaphon's soul (I.i.113), he wondered at it (120), a wonder intensified by Ford's addition to Strada, the flock of birds silent in wonder. Menaphon touches upon the beauty of the lutanist (ll. 115, 124) and concludes, not like Strada with a trite moral on the death of the bird, but with an association of the surpassing music of the lutanist with the surpassing 'music' of his moral and spiritual beauty (ll. 165–70). Finally, there is a significant addition to Strada; Ford's victor in the contest sheds tears of remorse at the death of the nightingale and attempts to smash the lute. Thus Ford introduces us to Parthenophill, to the play's mood and values, to 'Concord in discord, lines of differing method' that are at last to meet 'in one full centre of delight' (ll. 142–3).

In a marginal note to III.i.113–14 Ford refers the reader to Democritus Junior (Robert Burton's pseudonym, taken from the Greek philosopher Democritus, sometimes known as the laughing philosopher) thereby acknowledging his debt to Burton's *The Anatomy of Melancholy*, first published in 1621, and subsequently in 1624 and 1628, with five further editions before the end of the century, testimony to the popularity of the work. Scholars have studied the influence of *The Anatomy* on Ford's plays,[13] and so far as concerns *The Lover's Melancholy* he appears to have written the play with Burton's treatise at his elbow, to judge by the correspondences detailed in the commentary to this edition.[14] A preamble on Burton and his treatise will be helpful.

Robert Burton was in the first place a divine[15] and his interest in medicine was only one aspect of a scholarship that ranged over a vast field of interrelated disciplines. In the prefatory 'Democritus to the Reader' Burton tells us that he prefers divinity as the queen of professions to physic (p. 27), and although the omnium gatherum of curious scholarship and observation that follows might belie that claim, a fundamental religious bias is evident. Burton's conception of melancholy is that of a state that is all too often, as in the case of Lady Macbeth, more in need of the divine than the physician. Whole kingdoms that are irreligious, corrupt and tyrannical are regarded by him as being in a state of melancholy ('Democritus to the Reader' pp. 65–71). When he describes the causes and symptoms of melancholy states we are often confronted with a tirade against the self-indulgent excesses of passion and consequent criminal actions. The second partition, concerned with the cure of melancholy, includes a long 'Consolatory Digression containing the Remedies of all manner of Discontents', consolations of philosophy drawn from Christian and Stoic thought; the cure is spiritual. While Burton accepts that bodily disorders may work upon the mind to produce melancholy, and that such melancholy is to be pitied as coming from 'a more inevitable cause' (pp. 318–20; 1: 2: 5: 1), yet he regards much melancholy as not inevitable but proceeding from the indulgence of passions that can and should be controlled by reason. In writing of the will he opposes the Stoic view of fatal necessity, insisting here and elsewhere that the will has the power to do or not to do, 'Otherwise in vain were laws . . . rewards . . . punishments: and God should be the author of sin' (p. 146; 1: 1: 2: 11). On fatal necessity he writes, 'the Stars incline, but not enforce' (p. 810; 3: 2: 5: 5).

Whatever may be thought about the extent of Burton's influence on the ethical standpoint of Ford's plays it is impossible to agree with Sensabaugh that Burton saw the life of man as determined by immutable laws of cause and effect, and that Ford follows him in removing human activity from the realm of ethical choice.[16] The overall evidence of Ford's plays suggests agreement with one traditional strain in Burton's thinking, that reason should control passion.[17] This is obvious in *The Lover's Melancholy*; Menaphon, rejected by Thamasta, leaves Cyprus for a year that his love may lessen and she be free to marry another; Cleophila places the care of her father before her love for Amethus and he in return restrains his ardour, while Eroclea is a model of self-control and obedience. Conversely, Palador, however excusable his melancholy, is censured for his self-indulgence and neglect of princely duties (II.i.90–1, 134–5). Thamasta indulges her passion for Parthenophill conscious though she is of improper conduct (I.iii.79–82); the contrast between her and Cleophila is pointed. Burton's rejection of a fate that overrides freedom of choice is amusingly endorsed by Ford. Thamasta claims that her love for Parthenophil is pre-destined: "Tis a fate / That overrules our wisdoms' (I.iii.94–5); 'in vain we strive to cross / The destiny that guides us' (III.ii.135–6). The destiny could not be fulfilled because the man she loved was a woman. There is no necessary connection between Burton and the moral of this episode

INTRODUCTION 7

and yet her remark. 'O, the powers / Who do direct our hearts laugh at our follies!' (III.ii.181-2) might come from Burton, the 'powers' here being the Providence to which he is committed.

The third Partition of *The Anatomy* deals with love melancholy. Burton is primarily concerned with what he calls 'heroical love', a pathological state to be distinguished from married love which is natural and honourable, a distinction[18] which he makes in 3: 2: 1: 2. Heroical love is a degeneration to lust, a disease, a species of melancholy, begetting rape, incest, murder. Sensabaugh says that *The Lover's Melancholy* 'represents most completely [Ford's] almost morbid interest in heroical love', and that Palador is suffering from it.[19] In fact there is only one example of heroical love actually in the play, Thamasta's violent passion for Parthenophill which leads her into deceit, self-abasement, jealous fury and family discord, all of which is consonant with Burton's diagnosis. Equally consonant was the attempted rape of Eroclea by Agenor, antecedent to the play and cause of its major distresses. Palador is not properly to be defined as suffering from heroical love, but as a victim of love melancholy, an object of sympathy despite the censure of his advisers. The love of other characters in the play is honourable; they do not fly to the extremes of Agenor and Thamasta but patiently work to the consummation of marriage. What has been said so far is not to question the influence of Burton on *The Lover's Melancholy* but to clarify it. Indeed, in one respect, whether coincidental or not, Burton and Ford are close in the combination of divine and physician, for the therapeutic of the play operates within a clear ethical and Providential frame work.

Little is to be gained by trying to relate the characters of the play to particulars given in *The Anatomy*. The 'cases' of Palador and Meleander probably draw some details from Burton as, for example, the exercise, recreation and sleep recommended or applied for their cure, but the actual cure and the centre of interest in the play is the restoration of Eroclea. The conduct of Palador has no necessary dependence on Burton, and Burton himself drew upon his reading of fiction, as did Ford, for his observations. In describing the symptoms of lovers Burton wrote, 'Every Poet is full of such Catalogues of Love Symptoms' (p. 728; 3: 2: 3).[20] However, there is one character deserving of comment. Is Corax modelled on Burton?[21] Corax's real home – like Burton's – is the university, and in his distaste for court life (II.i.56–60; III.i.91–9, 131–8) when he could be at his studies he may be thought to resemble Burton, given the latter's addiction to scholarship and satirical slant on mankind. Corax is frequently referred to as a scholar, his medical skills being but part of his learning, as was the case with Burton. He refers to his masque in a deprecatory way as a 'scholar's fancy', asking Palador to view it indulgently as a non-professional university piece (III.iii.1–5).[22] Like Burton Corax is a bachelor (I.ii.117–18) and, significantly, he is referred to as 'humorous and testy', having, as 'men singular in art' always have, 'some odd whimsy more than usual' (III.iii.7–9). There is no reason to suppose that Ford ever met Burton but the characterisation of Corax is just such as a reader might derive of Burton from *The Anatomy*, an author eccentric, singular and 'humorous', one well aware that scholars are as absurd as the rest of mankind: 'Democritus, that common flouter of folly, was ridiculous himself' ('Democritus to the Reader', p. 94). Ford may have been gently poking fun at Burton in the irritable, bustling, self-important figure of Corax. Certainly, he is one of Ford's most engaging creations, and a useful astringent to over-sweetness; thus his sly irony when the therapeutic honours begin to shower on Meleander, 'There's one pill works' (V.ii.58).

The influence of Burton on Ford must be viewed in the perspective of several decades of interest in melancholy.[23] Timothy Bright's *A Treatise of Melancholie* (1586) was only the first of several psychological treatises before Burton, while the drama of the period furnishes a wide range of melancholy types which would fall within Burton's purview of manifold inordinate and distorted appetites. Ford's plays are shot through with reminiscences of earlier drama, Shakespeare being particularly evident.[24] With regard to *The Lover's Melancholy* critics have followed T.S. Eliot in drawing attention to the influence of Shakespeare's last plays.[25] It is not just the pattern of reunion after loss, especially that of Meleander and Eroclea, reminiscent of the reunion of Pericles and Marina, but also the sense of a Providential ordering of events, and of the achieved happiness still touched by the feeling of sorrows undergone. The clear virtue of Eroclea and Cleophila is like that of the young heroines of Shakespeare's last plays, and lying behind all is Cordelia. Cleophila has Cordelia's filial piety, and her relationship with her half-crazed father has its source in *King Lear*. Eroclea's restoration to Meleander echoes that of Cordelia; the music, the doctor's presence, the awakening from sleep, the fresh clothes, Meleander's belief that he is still dreaming. His lines beginning, 'My brains are dulled' (V.ii.231–6) recall Lear's, 'Pray do not mock me' (IV.vii.59–63). There may also be slight

INTRODUCTION 9

echoes of *As You Like It*,²⁶ and the masque of melancholy as a device to confirm what is suspected may have been suggested by Hamlet's 'mousetrap'.

The other Shakespearian play to which *The Lover's Melancholy* is indebted is *Twelfth Night*. In both plays a disguised woman becomes the object of another woman's love, and when Eroclea pleads on behalf of Menaphon, Thamasta's reply, 'Thou hast a moving eloquence', recalls the deep impression made on Olivia by Viola's eloquence on behalf of Orsino (I.v.248ff.). Thamasta's "Tis a fate / That overrules our wisdoms' (I.iii.94–5), when she finds herself falling in love with the young stranger, may have a connection with Olivia's 'Fate, show thy force: ourselves we do not owe' (I.v.294), just as there is a probable connection between the threatening behaviour of Menaphon and Orsino consequent on their belief that they have been deceived by a 'boy' (*Tw.N.*, V.i.123–5; *L.M.*, III.ii.204–6). Thamasta has Olivia's pride, while the love melancholy of Orsino may lie at the back of Palador's. Cuculus bears no resemblance to Malvolio but Grilla does refer to him as 'As rare an old youth as ever walked cross-gartered' (III.i.2).

Critics have seldom noted a relationship between Beaumont and Fletcher's *Philaster* (*c.* 1610) and *The Lover's Melancholy* although that relationship has recently been given detailed attention.²⁷ *Philaster*, like *Twelfth Night*, provides the general idea of the entanglements that beset a heroine disguised as a boy, but Ford also seems to have been influenced by a particular episode in *Philaster*. In I.ii Philaster describes how he first came upon the 'boy' Bellario seated by a spring and weeping over a garland of wild flowers, how Bellario told him of his parents' death and of his present pastoral existence. This pretty introduction of Bellario probably suggested to Ford a similar device for the introduction of the 'boy' Parthenophill, his use of the musical duel as the basis of Menaphon's account of his meeting with Parthenophill. The parallel is in dramatic device rather than detail, in similarities of situation between Bellario and Parthenophill, and in the note of pathos that is sounded.

The situation of a girl disguised as a boy, pining for her beloved and becoming the object of a woman's passion, is also found in Samuel Daniel's pastoral play *Hymen's Triumph* (1615). There is one telling particular not discussed by Robert Davril who mentions the play as one of the sources of *The Lover's Melancholy*.²⁸ Silvia, Daniel's heroine, destined by her father for a man she does not love, returns to Arcadia after two years' absence disguised as a boy.

Finding her beloved sunk in melancholy in the belief that she is dead, and not yet able to reveal her identity, she encourages him to believe that the lost one might yet be alive by telling him the story of a girl who returned safely home after strange adventures abroad, the circumstances of that story being exactly her own. This device is closely paralleled in *The Lover's Melancholy* except that here it is Rhetias and not the heroine herself who tells the story (II.i.187–212).

Melancholy states and their cure are the subject matter of other earlier plays as, for example, Fletcher's *A Wife for a Month* (1624),[29] *The Mad Lover* (1616) and *The Nice Valour* (Fletcher? 1616?); the two latter make use of masques in their attempts at cure. In Massinger's *A Very Woman* the physician Paulo, whose art like that of Corax is extravagantly praised, cures the 'Melancholy . . . near of kin to madness' (II.ii.80–1) afflicting Don Martino. The cure is effected by good counsel administered by Paulo as he appears successively to Martino in various disguises, the last being that of philosopher; he presents to Martino a good and evil genius who sing a song (IV.ii). Just as Palador reflects on 'man's fair composition' in musical terms (IV.iii.50–5) so does Martino (IV.ii.22–5, 158–9), and although that may be too commonplace to be of significance the theatricality of Paulo's therapeutic method is suggestive of that of Corax.[30] On a less elevated plane Massinger's *The Parliament of Love* (1624) includes a court physician Dinant, who administers comical cures for male ardours directed at other men's wives. None of these plays was in print when *The Lover's Melancholy* was written, and only *A Very Woman* might be thought to have any direct relationship with Ford's play. They represent one element in the theatrical fashions of the period which Ford developed as a major and more serious concern in *The Lover's Melancholy*.

Only in a loose sense can one speak of sources for the play. Ford wrote towards the end of a long and varied dramatic tradition which had soaked into his consciousness, and his plays are full of reminiscences. It is partly because of its eclecticism that *The Lover's Melancholy* has such an individual flavour. The play – to risk an over-simple analogy – inherits a mind from Burton, a body from Fletcher and Massinger and a soul from Shakespeare.

3. DRAMATURGY

In its story and in its moral substance *The Lover's Melancholy* is a distinctively harmonious play, and musical analogy springs to mind

INTRODUCTION   11

in considering its structure. The play is carefully patterned out[31]
with recurring motifs, counterpoint and varied recapitulations. The
melancholy of Palador is repeated in that of Meleander, just as the
process of each cure includes a spectacular scene (III.iii, IV.ii), while
his frustrated love has counterparts in Menaphon and Amethus. The
pride and self-will of Thamasta is contrasted with the humility of
Cleophila, and her rejection of Menaphon as beneath her in station is
balanced by the steady love of her brother Amethus for Cleophila,
the cousin of Menaphon. Thamasta is seized by a violent passion for
the lowly stranger Parthenophill only to be rejected as she had
rejected Menaphon. The pathos of the heroine disguised as a boy is
reversed in the comedy of Grilla, the page disguised as a girl, and that
parody of the main action is extended in the scene in which Grilla
apes the characters of Kala, Cleophila and Thamasta (III.i). Such
patterning of character and situation is carried into details. In III.ii
Menaphon watches, unseen, Thamasta's courtship of Parthenophill,
discordant in itself and in its results, and a variation of this occurs in
V.ii when we learn from Palador that he had been listening, unseen,
to 'passages of your united loves', the reunion of Meleander's family.
Discord and concord are pointed by other repetitions and balance.
In the first half of the play there are successive variations on court
and commonwealth disorders by Rhetias (I.ii.1–21), Sophronos
(II.i.1–16) and Corax (III.i.91–9); in the second half the reconciliations are heralded by striking arias, or meditations, on the harmony
of human personality (IV.ii.134–45, IV.iii.44–55), followed by the
exorcism of sorrows in the song which awakens Meleander to the
threshold of honour and joy (V.ii.1–10). Again, the discord/concord
idea is enforced by three set-pieces; the musical duel, an image of
both discord and concord, the grotesque masque showing the
discords of the mind, and finally the theatrical formalities through
which concord is restored to the mind of Meleander.

The symmetrical pattern of recurrence and variation can be traced
in other details. Amethus tells Menaphon that Palador will 'Gaze
upon revels, antic fopperies, / But is not moved' (I.i.74–5), and we
then learn that Corax is planning another device to try how that will
'move' the prince (I.ii.155–6); by this the prince is, indeed, 'throughly moved' (IV.iii.1). To demonstrate his continued love for Eroclea
Palador shows Rhetias a miniature portrait of her that he has
treasured (II.i.220–2), and it is Eroclea's possession of a miniature of
Palador that finally convinces him of her identity and love
(IV.iii.129ff.); the miniature of Eroclea is used to prepare

Meleander's mind for the restoration to him of Eroclea (V.ii.72ff.) and finally Palador gives that miniature to Meleander in exchange for Eroclea herself.

That preparation of the mind of Meleander illustrates what is central to the play's therapeutic (see below, pp. 19–21). The mind of the audience must also be prepared and informed, and Ford's skill in this is well illustrated in the play's first scene. The return home of Menaphon is initially dealt with in two nicely contrasted passages, Menaphon's satire of the foppish Pelias followed by his reunion with his father and his friend, Amethus, a feeling exchange in which the pieties of such relationships are portrayed. Once alone the two friends can unburden their hearts, first in an emotional but manly avowal of a soul kinship, then, as would naturally follow, Amethus tells Menaphon about affairs in Cyprus of deep concern to them both. Thus the audience is informed about the situation in Cyprus, characters and relationships. Naturally, again, Amethus enquires about Menaphon's travels and we learn of his encounter with Parthenophill in Greece, the account of the musical duel being effectively interspersed with responses from Amethus. Finally, a question from Amethus enables Ford to recapitulate for the audience the play's principal concerns; Menaphon replies that Parthenophill was persuaded to come to Cyprus by what he had been told of

> The fame of our young melancholy prince,
> Meleander's rare distractions, the obedience
> Of young Cleophila, Thamasta's glory,
> Your matchless friendship, and my desperate love. (I.i.182–5)

Ford has done more in this colourful and varied scene; he has established the play's values in delicacy of feeling and moral rectitude, and has given in the musical duel a seminal image for the play – pathos, and concord in discord.

Ford's inventiveness in informing and guiding his audience can be seen in our introduction to Palador (II.i). The scene opens with Aretus and Sophronos discussing the dangerous state of the commonwealth, the 'antic' goings on at court, the improper conduct of Palador's father, and the mysterious lethargy of Palador. Corax enters with Rhetias and the court 'antics', the party Corax is to train for the masque to 'move' the prince. Their nonsensical chatter illustrates Sophronos' remark about the state of the court, while the silencing of their clamour makes the entry of the prince the more arresting. Corax ends a tirade against Palador's neglect of his prescriptions for health with the complaint that he is losing his wits in his endeavours, to which the prince coolly and amusingly replies, 'I believe it' (l. 66). Palador remains indifferent to further complaints until he is stirred by the remark that his subjects are talking 'oddly' of him (l. 77). His interest caught, he demands the opinions of those present, thus opening the way for information about his character. He gets, and accepts, frank opinion but rebuffs the flattery of Pelias; he ignores the babble of Cuculus and marks out the silence of Rhetias, 'You have not spoken yet' (l. 121), whereupon all quietly withdraw except Palador and Rhetias. Audience interest at this move is intensified by a rapid and enigmatic exchange between them, followed by Palador's dramatic realisation, 'Ha! are all stolen hence?' (l. 144). After that momentary alarm he seizes the opportunity, in secret, to gain information about his father which has evidently been withheld from him. Rhetias can now tell the audience about events antecedent to the play, matters necessary to their fuller understanding of the situation of Palador and Meleander. That account stirs Palador to an implied confession of his deep interest in the lost Eroclea, 'No hope lives then / Of ever, ever seeing her again' (ll. 181-2), the cue for Rhetias to tell his 'story' of misfortunes in love, parallel to those of Palador and Eroclea, which had a happy ending. This moves him to an open avowal of his continued love for Eroclea, the goal to which Rhetias had been cunningly directing him. The cure of Palador has begun. It is an 'information scene' of considerable dramatic resource.

A just estimate of the dramatic and psychological qualities of the play hinges very much on questions raised by the disguise of Eroclea. A later section, concerned with therapy, will consider why the true identity of Parthenophill was so long concealed from Palador. Two other questions confront us now. Firstly, when does the audience, and secondly, when do certain of the characters, realise that Parthenophill is Eroclea? In the play's first scene Parthenophill is placed at the centre of attention through the account of the musical duel, and a mystery is left as to his identity:

> Whence he is,
> Or who, as I durst modestly enquire,
> So gently he would woo not to make known;
> Only, for reasons to himself reserved,
> He told me that some remnant of his life
> Was to be spent in travel.   (I.i.172-7)

This looks like a deliberate clue; after all Eroclea could have lied and given a less equivocal account, or Ford could have avoided raising the question in this direct way. During his first appearance in I.iii Parthenophill says very little but the audience might well wonder why he betrays evident emotion, 'Are you well, sir' (l. 65), when Thamasta shows favour to Menaphon. In II.i Rhetias follows his account to Palador of Eroclea's misfortunes with a parallel 'story' which has a happy issue, and comforts Palador with the thought that the same might happen to Eroclea. Palador can make no actual connection between the two cases since he knows nothing yet of Parthenophill, but the audience does and might now suspect the common identity of the young lady (disguised as a boy) of this 'story' and Parthenophill. The young lady fled to Athens, and Parthenophill had told Menaphon that she lived in Athens; both were solitary, and the pointedly undisclosed circumstances of Parthenophill's decision to spend some time in travel might well be the disclosed circumstances of the young lady of Rhetias' 'story'.

One notes how Ford draws attention to the disguise of the young lady. Palador's only comment on the 'story' is, 'In habit of a man?', to which Rhetias replies, 'A handsome young man'. When, immediately following this strong focus on Eroclea, Parthenophill enters and is introduced to Palador the 'stranger' says little but, as in I.iii, Ford signals silent emotion as is evident from Thamasta's remark that he should not wonder at the melancholy of Palador (l. 263). The indicators of Parthenophill's emotion grow stronger in II.ii, her first meeting with her sister and distracted father. His misery wrings from her the cry, 'This sight is full of horror', and the scene ends with her manifest distress:

> *Cleophila.* This gentleman is moved.
> *Amethus.*   Your eyes, Parthenophill,
>   Are guilty of some passion.
> *Menaphon.*   Friend, what ails thee?
> *Eroclea.* All is not well within me, sir.   (ll. 145–7)

Menaphon's question indicates the discrepancy between Parthenophill's emotion and the polite commiseration one would expect from a stranger to these people, and a young man at that.

As regards the audience's awareness of the true identity of Parthenophill, I believe that Ford intended such realisation certainly by the end of II.ii, if not earlier in II.i after Rhetias recounts the 'story' of the young lady. Ford made no attempt to portray Eroclea as actively impersonating a young man, as is the case with

INTRODUCTION   15

Shakespeare's Rosalind and Viola. What one sees of Parthenophill is a disposition to silence, or a betrayal of feeling beyond what the situation would seem to justify; Ford positively encourages the playing of the role in such a way as to invite suspicion. My view has two consequences for evaluating the play; it resists the idea that Ford was after theatrical revelations, and it enlarges the play's range of dramatic ironies.

Which of the main characters of the play are in the secret? Rhetias knows since he accompanied Eroclea in her flight and returned with her to Cyprus (V.ii.163–8). Sophronos ought to know since he arranged the flight and return of Rhetias and Eroclea (V.ii.159–62, 191–9), but he never gives any indication of this. Indeed, he confesses that he is as mystified as Aretus about Parthenophill (IV.iii.2–4), and there would seem to be no point in his lying to Aretus since Eroclea is about to be restored to Palador and the secret open to all. However, it is more important to determine whether Corax knows since he has been regarded as a somewhat comic bungler whose elaborate stratagems have little to do with the actual cure of Palador and Meleander.[32]

The conversation between Corax and Cleophila at the beginning of Act V, concerning preparations for the awakening of Meleander to 'present blessings' (l. 14), clearly presupposes that Corax knew that the restoration of Eroclea was to be one of them. Cleophila had been informed of the true identity of Parthenophill at the end of IV.ii by means of Thamasta's letter, but Corax must have know before if we are to put a charitable construction on his conduct earlier in that scene. He would hardly have tortured Meleander with the story of a supposed daughter of his own, 'long / Absented from me ... / Snatched from me in her youth ... / She comes to ask a blessing' (IV.ii.88–91), if he did not know that Eroclea was about to be restored to Meleander. Only one scene intervenes between IV.ii and the masque of melancholy (III.iii), which strongly suggests that Corax knew then the true identity of Parthenophill when he singled out the 'young man' as an example of love melancholy.[33]

Early in the play Corax had enlisted the help of Rhetias in his masque, and Aretus is working with them since they have evidently planned to leave Rhetias alone to probe the cause of Palador's melancholy (II.i.26–9, 125.1). This he discovers but is enjoined to secrecy by Palador, and he respects this with regard to Aretus and Sophronos for we later find them questioning Corax about the cause of Palador's melancholy (III.i.101ff.). Corax feeds them with learned generalities making, as Sophronos says, the cause to seem doubtful and therefore a cure impossible. Whatever Corax knows he gives nothing away but is confident of success (ll. 127–30). Since his masque reaches its climax in love melancholy for which there was no impersonator Corax either suspects the nature of Palador's sickness or Rhetias has told him. The latter explanation is more likely. Rhetias could not against Palador's wishes make public his secret, but he could tell Palador's physician and let him devise the 'mousetrap' which will provoke Palador to an involuntary disclosure of his love sickness. This allowed, it is a small step to accepting that Rhetias informed Corax about the true identity of Parthenophill. It has already been argued that Corax knew it before the beginning of IV.ii, and the singling out of Parthenophill suggests that he knew when designing the masque.

Questions raised by the disguise of Eroclea are central to one's interpretation of the play. In my view the essential character of *The Lover's Melancholy* is not of concealed facts suddenly disclosed but a process of healing in which known facts are slowly disclosed. I assert this despite some mystification with regard to Aretus and Sophronos; Ford may have deliberately cheated here for local effects, or he may simply have been inattentive to certain improbabilities and contradictions.

The main plot of the play is slight to a fault, yet less faulty if we consider that external action is less important as a source of dramatic interest than in its mediation of human feelings and values.[34] This is certainly not a play to seize us by the throat however it may engage the heart, and some deficiency in strong dramatic conflict is an inevitable consequence of a design in which there is a shared goodwill to achieve one goal. That is not to say that individual scenes have not considerable dramatic life, especially so in the scenes concerned with Thamasta's infatuation with Parthenophill.[35] Such is obviously true of that in which Thamasta forces her love on Parthenophill, a situation charged for the audience by the knowledge that Parthenophill is Eroclea and that Menaphon is watching (III.ii). A scene less theatrical but more subtly dramatic is I.iii in which both make their first appearance. Thamasta has already met and become enamoured of Parthenophill and this concealed passion fuels the scene. It has got the better of decorum for she appears in eye-catching finery for which she is rebuked by Amethus (ll. 1–10), and he follows this up with a sarcastic attack on her pride and rejection of Menaphon. This must touch raw nerves for she is already being humbled by her

INTRODUCTION 17

passion for Parthenophill, and that consciousness powers the equally sarcastic riposte directed at her brother's love for the lowly Cleophila (ll. 26-34). The complication of her feelings is apparent as she turns compulsively to speak of Parthenophill:

> I have given
> Your Menaphon a welcome home as fits me;
> For his sake entertained Parthenophill,
> The handsome stranger, more familiarly
> Than, I may fear, becomes me; yet, for his part,
> I not repent my courtesies. (ll. 34-9)

Once mounted, her feelings gallop away in praise of Parthenophill until, as if realising the danger, she reins with,

> Menaphon
> Was well advised in choosing such a friend
> For pleading his true love. (ll. 46-8)

This is some satisfaction to Amethus but his reply, 'Thou'lt change at last I hope', is answered by her revelatory aside, 'I fear I shall'. This should be sufficient indication for the audience, and Ford immediately presses home the irony by the entry of Menaphon and Parthenophill, subjects of that change. Thamasta addresses herself to Parthenophill, and when Menaphon interposes with his innocent remark that her beauty is 'More lovely than all other helps of art / Can equal' (ll. 56-7), she snaps back,

> What you mean by 'helps of art'
> You know yourself best; be they as they are,
> You need none, I am sure, to set me forth. (ll. 57-9)

Poor Menaphon! He could not know that she is still smarting from her brother's remarks about her gaudy appearance, just as Amethus when he made them was ignorant for whose benefit she was thus dressed to kill. Surprisingly, after having given Menaphon that metaphorical slap on the face, she accepts him formally as a suitor. But sudden graciousness is born of self-interest as her earlier remark (ll. 46-8) indicates. She remains officiously attentive to Parthenophill but deftly gets rid of the party, her urgent need being to give vent to her feelings. The high hopes with which Amethus and Menaphon depart are ironically juxtaposed to her confession of love in a rapid exchange with Kala, a passion shot through with guilt and suspicion. The scene ends with Ford sowing the seeds of future developments, Kala's bid for Parthenophill and her betrayal of her mistress (ll.

89–92). The life of the scene derives from Thamasta's undercurrent of emotion, of which the surface effects are touchiness of behaviour, sudden shifts of feeling and direction. It is done with subtlety and economy, a small excursion into Ford's acknowledged province, the drama of the heart.

A comparable sequence is Thamasta's introduction of Parthenophill to Palador (II.i.244ff.); Rhetias, Amethus, Kala and Menaphon are present, and dramatic irony comes strongly into play. The audience knows, and no one else but Kala, that Thamasta is in love with Parthenophill; the audience knows, and no one else but Rhetias, that the secret of Palador's melancholy is his love for Eroclea; the audience has just been given good reason to suspect that Parthenophill is Eroclea. Thamasta's presentation of Parthenophill to Palador is thus spiced with interest in the complications of awareness and unawareness subsisting between the characters. It is alive with tensions more readily to be perceived in performance than in reading. It is theatrical in the best sense, for the play of hidden feelings between Palador, Parthenophill and Rhetias, and to a lesser extent Thamasta, that Ford has here contrived is properly understated in the dialogue and left for visual realisation by the actors.[36]

The masque of melancholy (III.iii) is theatrical in a bad sense despite its function in the treatment of Palador. Nonetheless, its climax explodes into dramatic life in which irony plays a part. The audience now knows for certain that Parthenophill is Eroclea since in the preceding scene she had been driven to reveal her sex to Thamasta, and when she spoke of 'The story of my sorrows, with the change / Of my misfortunes' (III.ii.168–9) two and two could never more easily have made four. Thus, when Corax delivers his trump card, choosing Parthenophill as an example of love melancholy, the audience appreciates that she really is so afflicted and provocatively brought to the attention of the man she loves. The moment has further ironic edge for Corax does not know that Thamasta had been 'entangled' by Parthenophill when he supposes,

> Admit this stranger here—young man, stand forth—
> Entangled by the beauty of this lady,
> The great Thamasta, cherished in his heart
> The weight of hopes and fears.   (ll. 98–101)

This is close to the mark as Thamasta, Eroclea and Menaphon are all too aware. Thamasta's haughty, 'Am I your mirth?' covers her embarrassment. Palador is not the only one to leave the scene in consternation.

INTRODUCTION 19

The drama of the passages I have been analysing demands close attention if it is to be appreciated, but other features of the play do not encourage that. Ford has weighted the slight action with colourful set-pieces during which the play seems to stand still, or but slowly advances, so that the verdict on reading it may well be 'static', 'undramatic'. An editor must not be over-indulgent in excusing his play but he may be allowed to guard against imbalance.

All critics of Ford agree that broad comedy is not his forte. No doubt Meleander and Cleophila needed a servant, and through him some varying of the pathetic mood would advantage their scenes. But one could do without the insensitivity of Trollio; his remark, 'I could clip the old ruffian; there's hair enough to stuff all the great codpieces in Switzerland' (II.ii.17–18), is jarringly out of key. The idea of Cuculus and his 'feminine' page is inherently comic and has obvious stage possibilities for the boy player of Grilla; their scene of mock courtship (III.i) is a rather too strenuous comic bid, although its Euphuistic parody and bawdry carry it well enough. Actually, the more successful comedy in the play derives from the principals. There is nice humour in the fact that after Rhetias has mocked others he meets his match in the flyting with Corax (I.ii). Corax is an endearing creation. His self-importance, amusing in itself, does not include stuffiness and he has a sense of fun:

Rhetias. Are thy bottles [urine bottles] full?
Corax. Of rich wine; let's all suck together.   (I.ii.152–3)

As a university man he doesn't think much of court life and is certainly not intimidated by it; he can address Palador as if he were a student rather than a prince (II.i.101–4). His brisk presence gives a fillip to the solemnities of Meleander's awakening: 'Morrow to your lordship! You took a jolly nap, and slept it soundly' (V.ii.15–16). The infatuation of the great Thamasta results in some comic incongruities. She decks herself out in unbecoming finery; she can gush like a school-girl, 'He talks the prettiest stories . . .' (I.iii.43ff.), and falls over herself in eagerness that no one but she shall tell the story of the musical duel (II.i.257–59). As with Corax it is a gentle, unobtrusive humour of character and situation, perhaps more natural than broad comedy to the mind revealed in the play's other perceptions.

4. THERAPY

Passions of violent nature by degrees
Are easiliest reclaimed.

Why, when Rhetias had ascertained the cause of Palador's melancholy, did he not at once restore Eroclea to him? That Palador had enjoined him to secrecy is a lame answer since that injunction would have no force in the event of Eroclea's immediate restoration. The answer to the question lies in the play's therapy for melancholy states; if they are deeply settled then the process, the play suggests, must be gradual. Rhetias begins it by shifting to the forefront of Palador's mind the suppressed fact and circumstances of his grief, and leading him on to talk about his love. Yet he still defends his hurt mind with the barrier of secrecy until the shock of the masque throws it down.[37] Confronting Palador with Parthenophill, Corax thrusts home: 'O, were your highness but touched home, and throughly, / With this—what shall I call it—devil'. Palador can bear no more but, significantly, pauses in his hurried exit to address Parthenophill, 'Wait you my pleasure, youth'. The secret is out and Palador must face it openly. Commanding anger and activity replace passivity, accompanied by an intense but uncomprehending desire to see Parthenophill again, 'For he is like to something I remember / A great while since, a long, long time ago' (IV.iii.29–30). That suggests a frame of mind now receptive to the possibility that Eroclea may not be dead, and Palador meditates upon a heart 'untuned' by her loss. Even so, the wound is not suddenly healed with the appearance of Eroclea and its festerings show in his resistance to the truth. The process is gradual, 'But let me by degrees collect my senses'. Eroclea produces her miniature and his mind at last clears. This gradual 'tuning' of the mind is probably intended in the cure of Meleander, although the effect is less satisfactory. In his case no action is required to ascertain the cause of his melancholy, nor to bring it out of suppression, and since the true identity of Parthenophill must remain a secret until her restoration to Palador has been effected Ford has the problem of what to do with Meleander meanwhile. Ford works hard at Meleander's obsessive grief in II.ii but the interest of the scene derives more from the reactions of Eroclea and the pain to which the love of Amethus and Cleophila is subjected. Between this scene and IV.ii, when Meleander next appears, Corax has already got to work on him, apparently to exacerbate his distraction. He comes roaring on, flourishing a poleaxe, and Corax faces him in a Gorgon mask. This, and the subsequent procedure of Corax, suggest that the therapy is to be purgation by indulgence of the diseased humour, for he encourages Meleander in his misanthropy and grief until the passion begins to burn itself out and Meleander submits to the

INTRODUCTION   21

necessity of patience, and comfort in the thought of death. He is then drugged by Corax for recuperative sleep. If this scene is intended as a necessary step in the cure of Meleander, that function is not so apparent as is the case with the 'steps' taken for the cure of Palador. A better parallel is to be drawn between the three scenes in which Palador is gradually brought to his reconciliation with Eroclea, and the single scene (V.ii) in which she is restored to Meleander. He thinks the honours that are first showered upon him are enchantments, but when given the miniature of Eroclea his resistance falters: 'Be they enchantments deadly as the grave / I'll look upon 'em; patent, staff, and relic'. His ensuing meditation on the miniature makes easy the transition to reconciliation with Eroclea herself.[38]

Of course, Ford is not writing a text book, and the treatment of Palador and Meleander would be implausible in real life. Even within the play fiction a different structure for the story of *The Lover's Melancholy* is conceivable in which reconciliation was not preceded by psychological preparation. Contemporary audiences were well used to psychological implausibility in happy endings, and Shakespeare in his last plays is more concerned with the moral, rather than psychological, dimension of what leads up to and makes fit their reconciliations. Moral fitness also concerns Ford but there is a shift in emphasis and interest. The slowness with which the play moves to its reconciliations implies that you cannot suddenly bring together persons parted for years—persons mentally disturbed, emotionally repressed or believed dead—and expect an instant happiness. The play's means, the particular degrees, are an allegory of a necessary slow process.

5. VALUES

Concord in discord, lines of differing method
Meeting in one full centre of delight.

The musical duel points us to the imaginative unity of the play, an intertwining of concord, discord and pathos. The music of both nightingale and lutanist is in itself harmonious and resolves its own discords, but the contest between them is a discord resolved only in the death of the bird, 'music's first martyr'. The discord of that martyrdom is muted and turned to pathos as the conqueror weeps for the untimely end of the innocent bird. The elements of that little story are also those of the play but differently compounded. The discords are within the minds of certain characters, and their resolution is joy, not death, because other minds are harmonious and mutually concordant. Pathos enters the musical duel at the end but it colours the main action of the play throughout, centred on Parthenophill and suffusing other characters.

With Parthenophill pathetic feelings are aroused by the tenderheartedness shown for the dead nightingale, and from the guiltless death of the bird itself, insensibly associated with the person of Parthenophill. Such feelings intensify as the audience slowly becomes aware of his true identity as the lost Eroclea. Her sufferings are evident in II.ii, when she remains almost silent during the ravings of her father, until her tears and distress invite general solicitude. Subsequently she is the innocent subject of Kala's malice and Menaphon's reproaches, and has to endure the passionate advances of Thamasta. Eroclea's restoration to Palador is far from unclouded joy. Oppressed by her sufferings, her thoughts are more on death than love, and she struggles piteously against Palador's disbelief. Her speeches to him are composed of long sentences that wind their way down to doom (IV.iii.57ff.); she hopes for no more than an acknowledgement of her constancy before sinking to her grave. When at last joyously received by Palador her answer is subdued, more concerned with the goodness of Rhetias and Sophronos, and with the health of her father, than with her own good fortune.

The pathos of guiltless suffering encompasses Palador, Meleander and Cleophila, who must endure the consequences of Agenor's crime. Cleophila is 'too grieved to think of love', too low 'In mine own fortunes and my father's woes' (II.ii.58, 136), to respond to Amethus, and sorrow runs eloquently through the monosyllables of their parting lines:

> *Amethus.* Sweet maid, forget me not; we now must part.
> *Cleophila.* Still you shall have my prayer.
> *Amethus.* Still you my truth.

Meleander, in the scenes of his distraction, harps constantly on death and that is understandable, but that the same strain should sound through his joy unexpectedly sustains the pathetic mood almost to the end of the play. As with Eroclea's reunion with Palador the weight of sorrows is not easily shed. 'The good man relisheth his comforts strangely' (V.ii.120) says Rhetias, and he is right.

> I thank thee too, Eroclea, that thou wouldst
> In pity of my age, take so much pains

INTRODUCTION 23

To live till I might once more look upon thee
Before I broke my heart.

Palador may tell us that 'Sorrows are changed to bride-songs' (V.ii.253), but sorrows, the play tells us, are not so simply exorcised. The influence of *Twelfth Night* is probably more than in some points of situation and character (see above, p. 9). The impingement of time upon the comic world of *Twelfth Night*, felt in such chill reflections as 'beauty's a flower' and 'pleasure will be paid one time or another', is beyond the narrower compass of Ford. Yet he goes his own way in intertwining sadness, giving us a play in which 'Rare pity and delight are sweetly mixed' (V.ii.172).

The musical duel is a seminal image of pathos, and also of the harmony that affords much of the play's delight. The sorrowful plights of its characters do not result from inharmonious agents within the play; Thamasta's behaviour is a temporary discord for which her underlying generosity amply compensates (V.i.35–111). For the rest, all is care for the afflicted. Even the comic figures work for the good cause by taking part in the masque, while the friendship of Amethus and Menaphon expresses itself in the furtherance of one another's love suits. The central harmony of the play is embodied in Eroclea and Cleophila, consisting in obedience, constancy and beauty; Eroclea's restoration to the court of Cyprus brings its inherent harmony to 'one full centre of delight'. With them harmony is a moral indicator. Menaphon makes an explicit connection in speaking of Parthenophill (I.i.166–9). In another striking passage Meleander describes the moral perfections of Cleophila in terms of cosmic harmony. 'The model of the heavens, the earth, the waters, / The harmony and sweet consent of times' (IV.ii.137–8) cannot match the excellence of Cleophila—or of Eroclea either, since Meleander adds, 'She had a sister too'. In the reunion of Palador and Eroclea the image of harmony is again employed, here with reference to the harmony of two souls, which is necessary to man's happiness (IV.iii.50–5). When Palador takes Eroclea in his arms he apostrophises her as 'thou banished peace' and thinks of Cyprus as being 'new-settled in thy welcome' (IV.iii.137, 144), confirming the harmony to soul and state that she restores.

The Lover's Melancholy can excite no argument about moral obliquity, a charge which has been levelled at *'Tis Pity* and *Love's Sacrifice* in particular. Platonic, Christian and Stoic values interweave in a strict code.[39] The proper respects of friendship, of love, of service are observed, or sharply reproved in their neglect. Such harmony of soul is the essential condition of all the main characters. In Palador and Meleander it is jarred to discord but restored by the goodness of others; the anger of Amethus and Menaphon is the just response to what is, or seems to be, a violation of pledges of love and friendship by Thamasta and Parthenophill. The abundance of such words as noble, honour, sincere, truth, duty, service, and their derivatives, indicate the play's system of values. The play has echoes of *King Lear* as well as of *Twelfth Night*; if the filial piety of Cleophila and Eroclea owes to Cordelia, so does the loving service of Rhetias to Meleander owe to that of Kent to Lear. Clearly, the play is without Shakespeare's moral complexity but that is not to say that it lacks fine shades of feeling. Ford gets his pieties right in reserving the last scene of the play for the restoration of Eroclea to Meleander, but it is a tribute to the graciousness of Palador that he plays only an assigned part in that process. He and his court remain off-stage so as not to intrude on the reunion of Meleander's family; when Palador does enter it is as a loving son not a prince. He raises Meleander from his knees and embraces him: 'Father, you wrong your age; henceforth my arms / And heart shall be your guard' (V.ii.209–10). Fine discrimination of feeling is nowhere more apparent than in Thamasta's generous apology to Cleophila, Cleophila's gentle denial of its necessity and Thamasta's quick sense that such humility is a reproach to her pride, however unintended by Cleophila (V.i.36–55).

Just as the play's system of values is optimistic and unequivocal so is the religion that underpins it. Calvinist doctrine of the elect has been noted in *Christes Bloodie Sweat* (1613), a poem generally thought to be by Ford, but elsewhere in the same poem the availability of salvation to all is implied.[40] However that may be, there is no sign of Calvinism in *The Lover's Melancholy*. Thamasta's references to unavoidable fate are a rationalisation of her misguided desires (see above, p. 6). Pious thankfulness to a sheltering Providence is the key-note. Cleophila's obedience is emblematic of what man's relationship to Providence should be; in Palador's words,

> We are but fools
> To trifle in disputes, or vainly struggle
> With that eternal mercy which protects us.   (IV.iii.134–6)

That does not mean passivity, such as we find in the elect Charlemont of *The Atheist's Tragedy*. Ultimate happiness, as in Shakespeare's last plays, is not just the act of Providence; its designs are effected by the goodness of man deriving from, and working with, Providence.

Palador is commissioned by the powers of heaven (V.ii.100–1), but he needs to be 'circled, with a guard / Of truly noble friends and watchful subjects' (V.i.150–51). That harmony overarches the play.

In discussions of Ford it is sometimes asked how he was influenced by the cult of Platonic love associated with Queen Henrietta Maria that emerged in the late 1620's.[41] To what extent it influenced *The Lover's Melancholy* is hard to say since the Platonic equation of beauty and virtue, such as we find in Eroclea and Cleophila, and the exalted soul-friendship of Amethus and Menaphon, go back to Spenser and the Italian neo-Platonists. Moreover, the idea of heterosexual love remaining Platonic does not arise in this play, as it does in *Love's Sacrifice* and *The Fancies*. Despite the sometimes strained courtliness of the love sentiments and a touch of religiosity—'The incense of my love-desires are flamed / Upon an altar of more constant proof' (IV.iii.89–90)—there is no religion of love in the play, but rather a love that is religious in dimension. The description of Cleophila as a 'heaven on earth' (V.i.102) has the ethical force of the whole play behind it.

6. STYLE

The grave piety, the restraint, the sensitivity of feeling of the serious parts of *The Lover's Melancholy* are mediated by a style whose features are, for the most part, those commonly noted in Ford's writing. The consensus of opinion appears in such phrases as 'weighted simplicity',[42] 'exceptional clarity and simplicity',[43] 'extraordinary simplicity and directness of expression'.[44] That style is noted as applying especially at moments of intense feeling, its constituents being direct rather than metaphoric statement, preponderance of monosyllables, verbal repetition, balanced phrases:

Palador. But what became of fair Eroclea?
Rhetias. She never since was heard of.
Palador.   No hope lives then
       Of ever, ever seeing her again.
                                                    (II.i.180–2)
Eroclea.   I must not blush
   To let Prince Palador, if I offend,
   Know when he dooms me, that he dooms Eroclea.
   I am that woeful maid.   (IV.iii.116–19)

That economy and restraint of language, where over-charge of feeling moves towards expressive silence, is quintessential Ford. But such moments of distillation are relatively infrequent and should not be pressed into service as if they told the whole story. Directness and simplicity are terms needing scrutiny in their application to *The Lover's Melancholy*. They are useful pointers to the sparseness of metaphor, or at any rate of metaphorical complexity, and to colloquialism ('Good, give me leave, I will sit down indeed; / Here's company enough for me to prate to'), but they can be misleading. Davril, writing of Ford's style generally, notes the frequency of substantives of Latin origin, abstractions often of moral and intellectual rather than emotional content; he notes also that abstractions are grouped together, or coupled with concrete terms in unusual ways that can make the sense difficult to grasp.[45] Such characteristics are certainly present in *The Lover's Melancholy* and, while producing little obscurity, they sometimes contribute to an effect which is not direct or simple, but courtly, formal and even syntactically strained. This is especially apparent in the exchanges between Thamasta and Eroclea in III.ii and between Palador and Eroclea in IV.iii.

> time
> And safe experience have so throughly armed
> My apprehension with a real taste
> Of your most noble nature, that to question
> The least part of your bounties, or that freedom
> Which heaven hath with a plenty made you rich in,
> Would argue me uncivil; which is more,
> Base-bred; and which is most of all, unthankful.   (III.ii.69–76)

The opening circumlocution for 'I have learned to be confident of your noble nature' is strangely expressed in an 'apprehension' being 'armed' with a 'taste'; the dependent clause of ll. 72–4 is double-barrelled and has in the following line its own dependent clause qualifying 'freedom'; the sense is suspended through the complex sentence until 'Would argue me uncivil', all the preceding lines being its subject. A similar strained effect is seen in

> Yet so much
> The difference between that height and lowness
> Which doth distinguish our unequal fortunes
> Dissuades me from ambition, that I am
> Humbler in my desires than love's own power
> Can any way raise up.   (III.ii.97–102)

The suspended sentence is top-heavy with its extended subject.[46] In a strange combination of the abstract and concrete Palador speaks of a 'neighbouring greatness' seducing a 'free-born resolution' (IV.iii.82–3); so also Menaphon speaking of his ambition,

> That durst to soar so high as to feed hope
> Of any least desert that might entitle
> My duty to a pension from your favours. (IV.i.49–51)

Such syntactical complexity and use of abstraction, together with the elevation of sentiment, have a distancing effect and tend to intellectualise emotion. In that linguistic context even Ford's much praised moments of extreme simplicity may be subtly modified in the impression made on us, certainly not appearing as intellectually contrived, but as feeling rarefied to an existence almost beyond flesh and blood characters. Sargeant remarks that although Ford was born in Devon and probably spent his childhood there we find little in his plays of nature and outdoor life, most of his scenes being indoors in palaces and castles.[47] That is true of *The Lover's Melancholy*, but the further point is to be made that there is a paucity of social or common-life references in the speech of the nobility with the exception of Meleander. As his despair contemplates man's pride, folly and deceit we are given a sense of a teeming and colourful society outside the confines of the play (II.ii.86–97, 109–17; IV.ii.65–70, 77–85; V.ii.43–7). For the rest, common-life references are mostly found in the comic scenes, the masque and some speeches of Corax and Rhetias. That the language of the high-born characters in general lacks this element is consonant with what has already been remarked of courtliness and strain in their speech. The overall impression is of a certain remoteness from the pulse of daily living. In addition, although some lines have one or two extra syllables, Ford is generally regular in his use of the iambic pentameter line and, successful though this is for gravity and control of feeling, the predominantly level beat tends to flatten out speech rhythm. For the effect of real speech Ford relies upon directness of expression and variation of phrasing through internal pauses:

> My Menaphon, excuse me; I grow wild
> And would not willingly believe the truth
> Of my dishonour. She shall know how much
> I am a debtor to thy noble goodness
> By checking the contempt her poor desires
> Have sunk her fame in. Prithee, tell me friend,
> How did the youth receive her? (IV.i.17–23)

This is efficient enough but a little stiff, formal rather than familiar. When syntactical complication and abstractions are also obtrusive that effect is insistent, a distancing of character and situation. The medium is the message with the speech of the nobility, elevation of sentiment and extremes of feeling. Ford's sensibility appears to be aural and intellectual rather than visual and concrete, as may be seen from the relative infrequency of metaphor. The musical duel and the 'arias' concerning harmony show the bias—as also perhaps does the symmetrical ordering of the play. Except in such passages his metaphorical writing is not memorable, but is sometimes vaguely apprehended, lacking in specific realisation (e.g. I.iii.2–6, IV.iii.75–80).

Those aspects of style I have been considering enter into our sense of the human experience given by the play but they should not be allowed to distort judgement. What it fails to give in certain kinds of verisimilitude it makes up for in concentration of focus, and within their own world of experience the noble characters live intensely. And, of course, theirs is not the only living; the 'lighter mixtures' sufficiently relate the play to the mundane, even if they were for Ford the 'bye' and not the 'main'.[48]

7. THE PLAY AND FORD'S EARLIER WORKS

The high moral tone of the play reflects that of his prose pamphlets, *The Golden Mean* (1613) and *A Line of Life* (1620), with their mingling of Christian and Stoic thought. If the ideas were traditional they were sufficiently strongly held to permeate *The Lover's Melancholy*. Eroclea and Cleophila exemplify the control of passions lacking in Thamasta, and fortitude in the face of adversity; their sorrow is undeserved, but her plight is of her own making and she must put matters right by repentance. In *A Line of Life* Ford considers man's responsibilities to himself and to society; a public man must first be a good man, disinterested in his service of society, not subject to flattery, self-seeking and licence. Palador has gathered about him such good counsellors; Aretus and Sophronos are suspected of self-seeking ambition (II.i.12–15) but they are men of integrity. They fearlessly give Palador their opinion of his conduct in contrast to the flattering Pelias; Palador is censured for the indulgence of his feelings at the expense of his state duties. Yet he is a sick prince not an evil one, and there is an implicit contrast between him and his father, Agenor, who committed injuries against truth and honour, encouraged by 'bad agents'; *A Line of Life* inveighs against flatterers who will entice a prince to lust after chaste beauty (vol. III, 403–4). The same pamphlet tells us that 'we were not born to traffic in follies . . . to revel in the apishness of ridiculous expense of time' (*ibid.*, 395), sentiments echoed by Rhetias (I.ii.1ff.) and Meleander (II.ii.86ff.); that there is little in the play to justify them would seem to demonstrate their importance to Ford. The poem, *Christes Bloodie Sweat* (1613), attacks the deification of sexual love and distinguishes between lust and lawful love. Such ideas are especially relevant to *'Tis Pity* but even in *The Lover's Melancholy* it was lust that precipitated the play's sorrows, and Amethus is careful to insist that *his* love for Eroclea's sister is pure, 'Without all mixture of unnoble thoughts' (II.ii.134).[49]

So far as concerns the collaborative plays with which Ford began his dramatic career—and his contribution to them cannot be assessed with any certainty—there is little indication of what is to come in *The Lover's Melancholy*, with the exception of *The Sun's Darling* (1624) in which Ford collaborated with Dekker.[50] In form it is a combination of morality play and masque. It opens with Raybright, 'the sun's darling', sunk in lethargy through discontent with his life, and he is admonished (cf. the censure of Palador, II.i.90–1) by the Priest of the Sun,

> 'Tis melancholy and too fond indulgence
> To your own dulled affections sway your judgement;
> You could not else be thus lost.   (I.i, vol. III, 111)

The Sun grants his wish that he may be allowed to enjoy for one year the pleasures of each of the four seasons, but Raybright is constantly drawn away from their delights by Folly and Humour. Finally, in a speech which anticipates many phrases and ideas in *The Lover's Melancholy*, he is scolded by the Sun for his frailty and admonished not to 'Question the power of supernal greatness' since,

> Man hath a double guard, if time can win him,
> Heaven's power above him, and his own peace within him.
>   (V.i, vol. III, 169)

In *The Lover's Melancholy* characters learn after their tribulations are over not to question Providence, and they have the same double guard, of Heaven and harmony of soul, achieved or re-achieved. The Sun's speech refers to the ordering of the world by the four elements, and to that of man's body by the four complexions or humours; Raybright had been in a disordered state of mind, referred to as melancholy, in the first scene, and one recollects that a disordering of the humours could be a cause of melancholy states. Raybright and Palador are very different characters but they may have grown from the same germ of an idea.

Ford used masque elements in many of his plays but, although this was a common enough feature in the drama of the period,[51] the masque in *The Lover's Melancholy* is unusually extensive, certainly in comparison with Ford's practice in his other plays. *The Sun's Darling* has pronounced masque characteristics in its many songs and dances, and the Sun's admonitions in the last speech of the play are preceded by a dance of eight masquers representing the four elements and the four complexions. After the masquers are revealed, and before they dance, Conceit explains briefly which element is being impersonated, while Detraction comments on each in much the comic-mad vein employed by the impersonators of states of melancholy in *The Lover's Melancholy*. The masque in *The Sun's Darling* is the contrivance of Conceit who introduces it with a long explanatory speech; Corax is the contriver in *The Lover's Melancholy* and he makes explanatory comments as the masque proceeds. We seem to have evidence of the re-working of a motif. In sum, whatever Ford's share in *The Sun's Darling*, in both form and moral ideas it has its place in the genesis of *The Lover's Melancholy*.[52]

8. TRAGICOMEDY

My view that *The Lover's Melancholy* is Ford's first independent play is open to question (see above, pp. 1–3) but scholars generally accept that it precedes his other tragicomedies, *The Lady's Trial*, *The Fancies* and *The Queen*. His use of the form developed out of that established by Fletcher and continued by Massinger, but Ford's practice differs from theirs in some important respects.[53] Although there is a moral earnestness in Massinger lacking in Fletcher, the tragicomedies of both are essentially theatrical. Their subject-matter is love and sexual intrigue, explored through crowded actions, improbable and sensational incidents, designed to place characters on an emotional rack and achieve the maximum in suspense and surprise. The happy endings have more of contrivance than inevitability especially where, as is often the case with Fletcher, they depend upon the revelation of a secret withheld from characters and audience. Whatever may be said of improbable events in *The Queen* or the last-minute revelation in *The Fancies* (in any case, a secret kept for moral purposes), Ford's tragicomedies do diverge from this pattern. External action in them is generally slight and Ford concentrates his attention on states of mind.[54] Certainly he places his characters in situations of emotional stress but it is the quality of response, especially dignity and self-control, that is important, finely achieved in Auria of *The Lady's Trial*. His happy endings are not chance, contrivance or merely Providential, but result from human worth and endeavour. Such endeavour is that of Rhetias and Corax, and that of Muretto in *The Queen* who cures Alphonso of his misogyny. The unshakeable rectitude of those who stand, and the sincere repentance of those who fall, lead these plays to their happy conclusions.

It is easier to group *The Lady's Trial*, *The Fancies* and *The Queen* together than it is to place *The Lover's Melancholy* with them. For one thing, sexual problems—jealousy, infidelity, misogyny—are their substance, whereas the substance of *The Lover's Melancholy* is the healing of wounds caused by an action anterior to the play. Like *The Tempest* it amplifies the content of a last act into a whole play; in a way *The Lover's Melancholy* is an extended reconciliation sequence. Again, *The Lover's Melancholy* is a Providential play whereas his other tragicomedies are not. And despite the virtue of such typically Fordian ladies as Spinella, Castanna and Castamella, they do not have quite the gravity and piety of Eroclea and Cleophila. The concerns of its serious action are unmerited suffering, loss and separation; there is sufficient in the play to assure the audience of a happy issue, but suffering and despair are strong, and correspondingly thanks to heaven are fervent. Three of Ford's tragedies were published in 1633, and the fourth, *Perkin Warbeck*, in 1634, and any of these may have been composed several years earlier, close to the writing of *The Lover's Melancholy*. Perhaps there is a pointer here to the gravity of the serious action of the play, to the hopeless note often sounded. In its emphasis on self-control and duty, and in its pathos, which echoes that of Penthea, it is certainly close to *The Broken Heart*.

Ford does not present a tragicomic vision of man as an incongruous mixture of the sublime and ignoble,[55] and his tragicomedies might be accused of sentimentality and over-simplification of the problem of evil. In *The Lover's Melancholy* Ford keeps evil agents outside the play; in Shakespeare's last plays, to which *The Lover's Melancholy* has been related, evil is an active presence, and in range of moral reference—the impingement of political and social responsibilities on personal dilemmas, and the sense that not the individual plight but the human condition is being examined—they quite outreach *The Lover's Melancholy*. Yet for all the narrowness of its focus, the Arcadian goodness of its characters, the play has its own peculiar shadows. Part of Shakespeare's tragicomic vision is the abiding sense of a cost that leaves its scars, of a world in which similar struggles may have to be fought again. In *The Lover's Melancholy* no palpable dragons are in sight nor are any in prospect, but the hesitant joys of its reconciliations tell their own story of the suffering and doubting happiness of the country of the mind. The play affords—for that period—a new perspective on human suffering, not simply in its concern with pathological mental states, but in its witness to depths of inward experience which may not readily be gauged from outward demeanour. The tragic potential of this Ford explored in *The Broken Heart*. It lingers as an after-taste to the bride songs of *The Lover's Melancholy*.

9. STAGE HISTORY

Subsequent to the original productions of *The Lover's Melancholy* at the Globe and Blackfriars immediately prior to its publication in 1629 only one other professional production is recorded, 28 April 1748, at Drury Lane for Mrs Macklin's benefit (originally planned for 22 April). There were further performances on 5 May and 20 May, the first of these being heralded in the *General Advertiser* for 3 May: 'The last new Reviv'd Play, call'd *The Lover's Melancholy*, will be acted by particular desire next Thursday, at Drury Lane'.[56] The production was the occasion of what appears to have been an advertising stunt in which Charles Macklin alleged that the play was by Shakespeare. In April Macklin published two letters in the *General Advertiser* containing verses said to be by Thomas May and Endymion Porter, contemporaries of Ford, and extracts from an alleged pamphlet called, *Old Ben's Light Heart Made Heavy by Young John's Melancholy Lover*. In a supposed quarrel between them Jonson accused Ford of revising a play by Shakespeare which, with the connivance of Hemminge and Condell, he had stolen from Shakespeare's papers. The theft was supported by verses; thus 'Endymion Porter':

> Quoth Ben to Tom [Randolph], the Lover's stole,
> 'Tis Shakespeare's every word;

> Indeed, says Tom, upon the whole,
> 'Tis much too good for Ford.

The whole affair was exposed by Malone as Macklin's fabrication for the sake of publicity.[57]

The Lover's Melancholy and *The Broken Heart* were on a list of plays assigned to Davenant and the Duke's Company, 20 August 1668, but there is no record of Restoration performances. 'Not acted these Hundred years' wrote the *General Advertiser*, 12 April 1748, in announcing the Macklin benefit performance of *The Lover's Melancholy*.

One of the Folger Shakespeare Library copies (11163, copy 3) of the Quarto of *The Lover's Melancholy* was at some time being prepared for a production, although there are no signs that it was ever actually used in the theatre. The preparation consists of cuts, marked by rough ink lines, amounting to one fifth of the text, and a list of dramatis personae written down the left-hand side of A2v which cropping has reduced to the terminations of a few character names. Presumably the cast list was to have been added to the right. The major cuts consist of most of the 'musical duel', the whole of the masque of melancholy scene and the comic material concerning Cuculus and his 'feminine' page, Grilla. Clifford Leech has detailed and analysed the cuts and markings;[58] such evidence as these afford points to a seventeenth-century, post-Restoration, dating. Whether or not the abridgement is to be associated with Davenant's revival of pre-1642 plays, the project seems to have been abandoned.

To be neglected by the theatre has been the fate of Ford's plays generally, with the exception in this century of *'Tis Pity*.[59] *The Lover's Melancholy* is not a strong contender for revival although its appeal to a modern audience would, I think, be greater than that of Ford's other tragicomedies. I have tried to indicate something of the play's dramatic quality and potential; the roles of Corax, Thamasta and Eroclea, in particular, offer scope to players. Given careful pruning and direction of the masque, an academic audience at least could be persuaded to accord a performance more than dutiful applause.

10. TEXT

The play was entered in the Stationers' Register 2 June 1629:

Henry Seile Entred for his Copie vnder the handes of Sir HENRY HERBERT and master Weaver *The lovers Melanchollye* by IOHN FFORD gent[leman]... vj^d/

It was published in the same year with the following title page:

THE / LOVERS / Melancholy. / [rule] *ACTED* / AT THE PRIVATE HOVSE IN THE BLACKE / FRIERS, and publikely at the Globe / by the Kings Maiesties Ser- / uants. [two rules] LONDON, / Printed for *H. Seile*, and are to be sold at the Ty- / gers head in Saint *Pauls* Church-yard. / 1629.

The Huntington Library copy bears the variant imprint,

London, Printed for *H.S.* 1629.

Collation: 4°, A–M4. There was no other early quarto and the play was not printed again until the nineteenth century.

Of the twenty-eight copies of the Quarto known by me to be in existence twenty-two were collated for this edition: Bodleian Library (five copies); British Library (three copies); Columbia University Library; Eton College; Folger Shakespeare Library (three copies); Glasgow University Library; Huntington Library; National Library of Scotland (two copies); Newberry Library; New York Public Library, Arents Collection; Victoria and Albert Museum, Dyce Collection (two copies); Yale University Library. The Eton College copy wants M4, and a Bodleian copy (Malone B 166 (10)) wants M3, M4, and is in other respects imperfect.

All the copies collated have the variant running title, *The Melancholy Louer*, on D3r, E1r, E2r, E2v, E3r, E4v, F2r, G1r, G1v, G2r, G3v, G4r, and pages 50, 51, 54, 55 are incorrectly numbered 66, 67, 70, 71. There are some confusions of prose and verse, and some variations in character names and speech prefixes, but in general the text is a good one, verbal errors being relatively few and minor.

Printing and composition

Sheet A contains the preliminaries and is printed on paper unlike that used for sheets B–M containing text and Epilogue (M4r),[60] which suggests that sheet A was printed last. The pattern of skeleton formes is difficult to establish with certainty since individual settings of running titles are not easily to be distinguished, but it seems likely that seven skeletons were used, and the table below indicates the probable pattern.

Sheets	Outer forme	Inner forme
B	1	2
C	2	1
D	3	4
E	5	3
F	6	3
G	3	5
H	7	3
I	3	7
K	7	3
L	6	7
M	6	3

} 3 Skeletons

For sheets B–C two skeleton formes were set, a new title being added to C inner since B outer had no running title on B1r, the first page of the text. For sheet D seven of the titles of these skeleton formes were re-used, with two titles transposed from one forme to the other, and vice versa, and one fresh title set erroneously as *The Melancholy Louer* on D outer, thus forming virtually two new skeletons, skeletons 3 and 4. Skeleton 4, D inner, was not re-used and was presumably distributed. Skeleton 3, D outer, was re-used for E–F inner, G outer, and subsequently, with the one title corrected, for H inner, I outer, K and M inner. Skeleton 5, replacing skeleton 4, was set with all four titles as the erroneous *The Melancholy Louer* and used for E outer and G inner and then distributed, the mistake having been discovered. Skeleton 5 was replaced by skeleton 7 which was set for H outer and re-used for I inner, K outer, L inner. Skeleton 6, set for F outer, was re-used for L–M outer although why it was kept standing so long without use is a puzzle.

According to this analysis three skeletons were in use for sheets E–G and L–M which suggests that these sheets at least were set by formes in order to keep pace with the press-work. In fact, that all the sheets were set by formes is indicated by the wide variation in the spacing of character entries; some are cramped between lines of speech, some are allowed plenty of white space. It is unlikely that such variation could be solely attributable to differences between compositors, and in any case the variation does not fall into any observable pattern of stints. The spacing of entries seems to have been the principal means of repairing deficiencies in casting off. Certain other features of the text which might be explained by cast-off copy do not for the most part seem to be so explicable. As noted in the collation there are in the editor's judgement twelve examples of prose/verse mis-settings. Eight make no difference to the number of text lines and one lengthens by a line an already crowded page (F3r); only three might be attributed to the compositor's need to make up his page (D2r, G2r, M1v). Prose/verse mis-settings apart, there is also mis-division of verse on C1r and I2v, which increases the number of text lines, but the same effect could more easily have been achieved on C1r by increasing the space of the entry on the same page, and on I2v by increasing the space of the cramped entry on the compositorially consecutive I3r.

Another feature occurring throughout the text which might be thought to derive from cast-off copy is a difference in the setting of single-line verse speeches which follow a verse speech ending in a part-line. In some cases the line is correctly divided and set as two lines, in others it is set as a single line. An incorrect single-line setting saves one line, and although space saving might possibly account for some instances it certainly cannot explain all, since at least five examples of such setting occur on pages which have spacious entries and are in no way cramped. In sum, it would appear that entry spacing is the only clear evidence of cast-off copy, and explanation of the other features discussed must, in the main, be sought elsewhere.

The three-skeleton presswork suggested for some of the sheets, and the appearance of the erroneous running title in sheets D, E, F, G, strongly indicate composition by more than one compositor, but analysis has produced inconclusive results. In fact, there is much that seems to indicate setting by one compositor. There is no variation in the size of the printer's measure and catchwords are consistently treated. 'I'll', with one exception (I'le), invariably appears as 'Ile', and the apostrophe is never used for the possessive. There are only three exceptions to the spelling 'doe', and one each to the spellings 'goe' and 'here'. In the variation 'in-/en-' and 'im-/em-' at the beginning of words 'in-' and 'im-' are much favoured, but no pattern is observable and both forms sometimes occur on the same page. Proper nouns are invariably italicised, except geographical locations; these are normally in roman, and the few exceptions are not significant. Despite such findings, for what they are worth, the likelihood remains that more than one compositor was at work. However, the text is a good one and presents no editorial difficulties for which a knowledge of the particular habits of different compositors would be helpful.

Press correction was sketchy. Two corrections were made in the inner forme of sheet D (II.i.16–17, 148), and two in the outer forme of sheet H (III.iii.18, IV.i.53), but incorrect readings, the erroneous running title, and the mispagination are present in all the copies examined.

The Copy

The text derives from copy obviously prepared for publication, as is evidenced by the dedication and commendatory verses. Similarly, the Prologue and Epilogue, being of a literary rather than a theatrical character, were presumably added for publication. The list of King's Men players, the Latin marginal notes, and the Latin act headings and conclusions,[61] are also literary features. The text shows no signs of theatrical origin, the descriptive stage directions (e.g. for the masque) being of an authorial character. One feature of the text, found in the quartos of Ford's other plays, is the use of italic for purposes other than the conventional, i.e. for speech prefixes, songs, stage directions and proper nouns.[62] The words selected for italicisation are notably such as carry emphatic weight or emotional charge: e.g. *May-game*, I.ii.10; *praise it self*, I.iii.61; *Her*, II.i.166; *Man*, IV.iii.47; *Cruell-mercy*, IV.iii.85; *faire subtilty*, IV.iii.102; *simplicity, truth, Martyrdome, holinesse*, IV.iii.121–2. 'Melancholy' is generally italicised, as are the names of the kinds of melancholy in the masque, and a few other words of no obvious special significance. The use of italics (or roman where the text is in italics) to indicate emphasis is also found in the dedicatory epistle, commendatory verses and Epilogue. Given its presence in Ford's other quartos there can be no doubt that this feature derives from copy.

A text thus characterised, together with its general cleanness, suggests authorial or scribal fair copy, and the evidence slightly favours the latter. The variation in the setting of single verse speeches, and the prose/verse mis-settings do not seem for the most part to result from deficiencies in casting off and are more likely to derive from copy. Presumably authorial fair copy would have tidied up these features. The same may be said of the three character entries placed on the right side of the text rather than centred (B1v, C1r, G4v); this placing is unlikely to be deliberate or erroneous on the part of the compositor, and they were probably so placed in the copy, the author having omitted them and squeezed them in at the side of his manuscript. There are some variations, minor with one exception, in the spelling of character names, and also in speech prefixes. Some of these are doubtless compositorial, and some of the shorter forms of speech prefixes are due to line justification. But if some of these variations derive from the printing house, it is also very possible that some derive from copy. It is surprising to find the compositor setting *Menander* for *Meleander* (E4r, I1v), particularly on E4r (II.ii.7) where it is followed five lines later by *Meleander*. There is no way of knowing whether the Athenian playwright's name was running in the head of the author or of the compositor but the odds are on the former. It may be an instance of something which a scribe failed to correct. Scribal fair copy best fits what evidence there is although the case for authorial fair copy remains open. On this view a conservative approach to the text is indicated, and for the most part emendation has been confined to correcting prose/verse confusions and evident verbal errors, all minor. Q's punctuation is recorded in the collation where alteration has involved a change of sense. A long dash is frequently used in the punctuation of Q, not only where one character interrupts another, but also sometimes to signal a pause or break in thought, or the direction of speech to a particular character. It is also used at a few exits. Since these dashes seem likely to be authorial they have been generally retained and, if dropped, recorded in the collation. Dashes introduced by the editor are distinguished by being shorter. The colloquial "ee' for 'ye' is a characteristic form found in all Ford's plays and has been retained throughout.

A final point concerns Q's reading 'Coach' at V.i.18, V.i.178, and '*in a Coach*' at V.ii.0.1; all previous editors emend to 'couch' (see note to V.i.18) and '*on a couch*'. Such emendation assumes the compositor's misreading, three times, of 'a' for 'u' in the copy (and the alteration of '*on*' to '*in*' in the stage direction), but there is only one other example of such misreading, 'Rupture' for 'Rapture' at III.i.111. It is true that we find the variants *Pelias/Pelius*,

INTRODUCTION 39

Rhetias/Rhetius, *Aretas/Aretus* (among other minor variants in character names), but these may well have been in the copy. Authorial variation between '-as' and '-us' in the termination of names of classical derivation seems as likely as misreading of the copy. An alternative hypothesis to support 'couch' might be that the compositor (or possibly scribe) consistently altered to 'coach' because the idea of a stage couch seemed unusual. Yet 'coach' would be the more unusual. Whatever may be thought of the plausibility of Q's 'coach' readings I have retained them, in line with the general conservative treatment of the text.

NOTES

1 An account of Ford's life and works is given by Derek Roper in his Revels Plays edition of *'Tis Pity She's a Whore* (London, 1975), pp. xix–xxvi.
2 Sargeant, pp. 21–4; Davril, pp. 68–71.
3 Bentley, III, 440–2, 449.
4 Roper, *'Tis Pity*, pp. xxxvii–xli.
5 Roper, *'Tis Pity*, pp. xxv–xxvi.
6 Roper, *'Tis Pity*, p. xl.
7 See below, p. 5.
8 Oliver, pp. 47–9, and Dorothy M. Farr, *John Ford and the Caroline Theatre* (London, 1979), pp. 11–12, take this view.
9 See Sir George Hill, *A History of Cyprus* (3 vols., Cambridge, 1940–48), vol. I.
10 Isocrates, an Athenian orator, was widely published and translated in the sixteenth century.
11 See L. C. Martin's informative note in his edition of Crashaw's *Poems* (Oxford, 1927), pp. 438–40. Charles Lamb chooses the musical duel as his excerpt from *L.M.* and comments that none of the other English versions of Strada's piece can compare with Ford's for harmony and grace (*Specimens of the English Dramatic Poets*, London, 1808, pp. 235–6).
12 *Poems*, Introduction, p. xc.
13 See Ewing and Sensabaugh.
14 Not all the correspondences prove indebtedness to Burton and some may derive independently from a common stock of knowledge, but Ford's close attention to Burton is nonetheless evident.
15 In 1599, at the age of twenty-two, he was elected to Christ Church, took the degree of B.D. in 1614 and lived in Christ Church for the rest of his life, during which period he was vicar of St Thomas's, Oxford, and held livings in Lincolnshire and Leicestershire.
16 Sensabaugh, pp. 34, 70–1 and *passim*.
17 Cf. Stavig, pp. 69–70.
18 Stavig makes the distinction, pp. 72–3.
19 Sensabaugh, pp. 62, 75.

20 Bridget Gellert Lyons, *Voices of Melancholy: Studies in Literary Treatments of Melancholy in Renaissance England* (London, 1971), points out that Burton's reading in English literature was considerable, and that his library contained many plays by contemporary dramatists, including *L.M.* (pp. 114–15).
21 Sargeant notes this, but dismissively (pp. 78–9).
22 Burton himself wrote a Latin play, *Philosophaster*, which was performed by the scholars at Christ Church, 16 February 1617/18 (Bentley, III, 99–100). The play was not printed until 1862 but it is quite possible that Ford knew of it since some students would have moved from the university to the Inns of Court. A cast list is preserved but, unfortunately, without sufficient detail to trace names with certainty in Inns of Court records. Burton seems also to have shared in the authorship of the lost play, *Alba*, which was performed before James I in August 1605, at Oxford. See Richard L. Nochimson, 'Robert Burton's Authorship of *Alba*: a Lost Letter Recovered', *Review of English Studies*, N.S., XXI (1970), 325–31.
23 See Babb, *passim*.
24 See D. L. Frost, *The School of Shakespeare* (Cambridge, 1968), ch. IV, especially pp. 156–66; on the influence of Fletcher see A. C. Kirsch, *Jacobean Dramatic Perspectives* (Charlottesville, 1972), pp. 112–26.
25 *Selected Essays* (London, 1932; ed. cit., 1958), pp. 194–5. Cf. Leech, p. 107, Sargeant, pp. 117–18.
26 Small points are made by Oliver, pp. 52–3.
27 Dorothy M. Farr, *John Ford and the Caroline Theatre*, pp. 16–21. In omitting reference to *Twelfth Night* Farr rather overstates the influence of *Philaster*, but the comparison does good service to Ford's play in highlighting its moral purposefulness.
28 Davril, p. 152. There may be a verbal echo of Daniel's lines, 'Womens affections doe like flashes proue, / They oft shew passion when they feele small loue' (A2r) in Ford's, 'Women in their passions / Like false fires flash to fright our trembling senses, / Yet in themselves contain nor light nor heat' (IV.i.3–5).
29 There is a close parallel between Fletcher's, 'Come home again, my frighted faith, my vertue, / Home to my heart again' (IV.i; vol. V, 52) and Ford's, 'Come home, home to my heart, thou banished peace!' (IV.iii.137). It is echoed again in *The Fancies*: 'Come home again,—home, Castamela, sister, / Home to thine own simplicity' (IV.i; vol. II, 287).
30 It is thought that *A Very Woman* (1634) is a revision of a play by Fletcher, which must have been in existence before 1625, the year of Fletcher's death (see *The Plays and Poems of Philip Massinger*, vol. IV, 201–2). Since we cannot be sure that the original play contained the 'cure' scene (IV.ii), if there is a connection between that and Ford's masque of melancholy then Massinger and not Ford may be the debtor.
31 Oliver, p. 58, sees the careful balance of character and neat contrivance of incident as signs that this is Ford's first unaided play, although the same argument might be applied to *The Broken Heart*.
32 See Ewing, pp. 33, 39, 42. Other critics have viewed his skills as, at best, limited; e.g. Leech, p. 106, Ronald Huebert, *John Ford: Baroque English Dramatist* (Montreal and London, 1977), p. 61.

33 I know of only one critic who considers the point closely and he believes that Corax is ignorant throughout of the true identity of Parthenophill; see Anderson, pp. 54–5. K. P. Jochum, *Discrepant Awareness: Studies in English Renaissance Drama*, Neue Studien zur Anglistik und Amerikanistik, Band 13 (Frankfurt am Main: Bern: Las Vegas, 1979), does not include *L.M.* in his discussion of Ford.
34 See below on the play's therapy and values, pp. 19–25.
35 Leech, p. 107, oddly refers to Thamasta's infatuation as a 'rather tiresome complication of the serious action'; in fact, it contributes importantly to the dramatic and moral life of the play.
36 Sargeant observes that Ford's plays 'cannot be fairly judged by merely reading them, because he leaves to the actor his share of interpretation' (p. 155).
37 The function of the masque is seldom properly understood and Sargeant considers that its inclusion can hardly be justified at all since the cause of Palador's melancholy has already been revealed by Rhetias (pp. 74–5).
38 For a perceptive analysis of the play's psychology of symptoms and cure see Anderson, pp. 52–60, although his view that Corax is executing Ford's plans rather than his own seems to me mistaken.
39 On Ford's ethical thought see Stavig, pp. 20–35.
40 See Sargeant, pp. 10–11 and Leech, p. 23.
41 For opposed view see Sensabaugh, pp. 94–173, and Stavig, pp. 36–45. They agree that the cult influenced Ford but Stavig contests Sensabaugh's view of its libertine effect.
42 Clifford Leech, *John Ford* (Harlow, Essex, 1964), p. 11.
43 Oliver, p. 128.
44 Sargeant, p. 158.
45 Davril, pp. 429–35.
46 For similar effects see III.ii.115–23, 167–73.
47 Sargeant, p. 152.
48 Prologue, ll. 14–16.
49 Two other non-dramatic works, *Fames Memoriall* and *Honor Triumphant*, both published in 1606, have led scholars to discuss the orthodoxy of Ford's views on love and marriage. The issues are too complex to consider here, and in any case the question is not relevant to *L.M.*
50 The question of Ford's share in the play is hedged about with difficulties; see Oliver, pp. 37–41.
51 See Inga-Stina Ewbank, '"These pretty devices": A Study of Masques in Plays', *A Book of Masques*, general editors T. J. B. Spencer and S. W. Wells (Cambridge, 1967), pp. 407–48.
52 Anderson, p. 39, suggests that *The Sun's Darling* anticipates the pattern of ethical conflict in *'Tis Pity* and *Love's Sacrifice*, although neither in this nor in other respects does the play seem to me to be of significance in Ford's later development.
53 On such differences see Leech, pp. 101–4, and Oliver, pp. 122–4; F. H. Ristine's *English Tragicomedy* (New York, 1910) is a comprehensive study of the form, and Eugene M. Waith has written a special study, *The Pattern of Tragicomedy in Beaumont and Fletcher* (New Haven and London, 1952).
54 Cf. Ronald Huebert, *John Ford: Baroque English Dramatist*, p. 120: 'With Ford, the obstacles to erotic fulfilment are removed entirely from the

objective world and transplanted into the subjective experience of the lovers; the separations between the protagonists in *The Lover's Melancholy*, *The Lady's Trial*, and *The Queen* depend respectively on the delusions of melancholy, jealousy, and misogyny.'
55 See Cyrus Hoy, *The Hyacinth Room* (London, 1964), pp. 213–22.
56 *The London Stage 1660–1800*, Part 4: 1747–1776, ed. George Winchester Stone, Jr. (Carbondale, Illinois, 1967), pp. 43, 50, 52–3, 55.
57 See Sargeant, p. 171, Davril, pp. 55–8, Bentley, III, 450–1, Leech, p. 108.
58 'A Projected Restoration Performance of Ford's "THE LOVER'S MELANCHOLY"?', *Modern Language Review*, 56 (1961), 378–81.
59 For an account of Ford on the stage after 1660 see Leech, pp. 133–40.
60 Of the Epilogue Gifford remarks, 'This Epilogue does not appear in all the copies. Mr.Heber's has it not' (I, 121). Some existing copies lack the last leaf, M4, on the recto of which the Epilogue was printed; probably the copy Gifford refers to was imperfect.
61 Only the first three acts have the Latin conclusion.
62 See the discussions by Roper, *'Tis Pity*, pp. lxiii–lxiv, and Peter Ure in his edition of *Perkin Warbeck* (1968), pp. xviii–xxii.

THE LOVER'S MELANCHOLY

THE LOVER'S MELANCHOLY

The Scene
FAMAGOSTA IN CYPRUS

The names of such as acted

JOHN LOWIN [CORAX]	RICHARD SHARPE [AMETHUS]
JOSEPH TAYLOR [PALADOR]	THOMAS POLLARD [RHETIAS]
ROBERT BENFIELD [MELEANDER]	WILLIAM PENN [SOPHRONOS]
JOHN SHANCK [CUCULUS]	CURTEISE GRIVILL [PELIAS OR
EYLYARDT SWANSTON	TROLLIO]
[MENAPHON]	GEORGE VERNON
ANTHONY SMITH [ARETUS]	RICHARD BAXTER

JOHN TOMSON [THAMASTA]
JOHN HONYMAN [EROCLEA]
JAMES HORNE [GRILLA]
WILLIAM TRIGG [KALA]
ALEXANDER GOUGH [CLEOPHILA]

The ... acted] These were members of the King's company, Lowin and Taylor being the leaders of the organisation at this time. T. W. Baldwin's suggested assignment of roles (*The Organization and Personnel of the Shakespearean Company* (Princeton, 1927), Appendix III, pp. 366–8) is given in square brackets; these actors and their roles are further discussed in Bentley, Vol. II, *passim*.

The Epistle Dedicatory

To my worthily respected friends, NATHANIEL FINCH, JOHN FORD, Esquires; Mr. HENRY BLUNT, Mr. ROBERT ELLICE, and all the rest of the Noble Society of Gray's Inn.

My Honoured Friends,
The account of some leisurable hours is here summed up and 5
offered to examination. Importunity of others, or opinion of mine own, hath not urged on any confidence of running the hazard of a censure. As plurality hath reference to a multitude, so I care not to please many; but where there is a parity of condition, there the freedom of construction makes the best 10
music. This concord hath equally held between you, the patrons, and me, the presenter. I am cleared of all scruple of disrespect on your parts, as I am of too slack a merit in myself. My presumption of coming in print in this kind hath hitherto been unreprovable, this piece being the first that ever courted 15

The Epistle Dedicatory] *only in running-title on A2v in Q.*

1–3.] With the exception of Nathaniel Finch all these Gray's Inn men have known literary affiliations. John Ford was a cousin of the playwright, dedicatee of Ford's *Love's Sacrifice*, and author of a commendatory poem to his *Perkin Warbeck*; he is also the dedicatee of Thomas Jordan's *Poetical Varieties* (1637). Henry Blunt (Blount), later Sir Henry, is remembered for his travel book, *Voyage into the Levant* (1636); he addressed a commendatory poem to Charles Aleyn's *Battailes of Crescey and Poictiers* (1633), and both he and Robert Ellice addressed commendatory poems to Sir William Davenant's *Albovine* (1629). Concerning the literary circle which Ford, Davenant and these dedicatees seem to have formed, see Mary Hobbs, 'Robert and Thomas Ellice, Friends of Ford and Davenant', *Notes and Queries*, N.S., 21 (1974), 292–3.

6–11. *Importunity . . . music*] A paraphrase of this courtly passage may be found helpful: 'I do not run the risk of adverse criticism (i.e. by appearing in print) because emboldened by the requests of others or by my own high opinion of my merits. I am not concerned to please many people because I am not concerned to please the mob. But where there is equality of rank and education there is a fellowship in judgement which produces the most harmonious conclusions.'

12–13. *I . . . myself*] I am as free from any disrespect from you as I am confident of my own worthiness.

14–16. *My . . . reader*] Ford had already published poems and prose pamphlets (see Introduction, pp. 28–9) but *L.M.* was his first play to be printed.

reader; and it is very possible that the like compliment with me may soon grow out of fashion. A practice of which that I may avoid now, I commend to the continuance of your loves the memory of his, who, without the protestation of a service, is readily your friend, 20

JOHN FORD.

---

16. *like compliment*] i.e. of 'courting' readers with further publication of plays.

18. *avoid*] put an end to.

To my Honoured Friend, Master John Ford, on his Lover's Melancholy.

If that thou thinkst these lines thy worth can raise,
Thou dost mistake; my liking is no praise:
Nor can I think thy judgement is so ill,
To seek for bays from such a barren quill.
Let your true critic, that can judge and mend,   5
Allow thy scenes and style; I, as a friend
That knows thy worth, do only stick my name,
To show my love, not to advance thy fame.

George Donne.

---

4. *bays*] conqueror's garland of bay leaves.
quill] pen.
6. *allow*] approve.
9. *George Donne*] probably the second son of the poet John Donne although the son was a military man; he also wrote commendatory verses for *Perkin Warbeck*. His commendatory poems to Thomas Heywood's *Philocothonista, or, the Drunkard* (1635) and Philip Massinger's *Great Duke of Florence* (1636) show him to have been the friend of other dramatists.

To his worthy Friend, the Author, Master John Ford.

I write not to thy play; I'll not begin
To throw a censure upon what hath been
By th'best approved; it can nor fear nor want,
The rage, or liking, of the ignorant.
Nor seek I fame for thee, when thine own pen   5
Hath forced a praise long since from knowing men.
I speak my thoughts and wish unto the stage
A glory from thy studies, that the age
May be indebted to thee for reprieve
Of purer language, and that spite may grieve   10
To see itself outdone. When thou art read
The theatre may hope arts are not dead,
Though long concealed; that poet-apes may fear
To vent their weakness, mend, or quite forbear.
This I dare promise; and keep this in store,   15
As thou hast done enough, thou canst do more.

                                    William Singleton.

---

9. *reprieve*] save from corruption.

13. *poet-apes*] would-be poets, a common term of literary abuse. See Ben Jonson's *Epigram* LVI which makes much of the charge of plagiarism from the true poets, a matter about which Ford shows himself sensitive in the Prologue to *L.M.*

17. *William Singleton*] He joined Ford at the Middle Temple 24 October 1626 and his commendatory poem to *The Emperor of the East* (1632) addresses Massinger as friend and kinsman.

To the Author, Master John Ford.

Black choler, reason's overflowing spring,
Where thirsty lovers drink, or any thing,
Passion, the restless current of dull plaints,
Affords their thoughts who deem lost beauties saints;
Here their best lectures read, collect, and see   5
Various conditions of humanity
Highly enlightened by thy muse's rage;
Yet all so couched that they adorned the stage.
Shun Phocion's blushes thou; for, sure, to please
It is no sin, then what is thy disease?   10
Judgement's applause? Effeminated smiles?
Study's delight? Thy wit mistrust beguiles;
Established fame will thy physician be,
Write but again to cure thy jealousy.

         Hum. Howorth.   15

1.] Choler, one of the four bodily humours, if it became black or adust (burnt up), could cause melancholy (Babb, p. 24). Since it cannot be a source of reason, 'reason's overflowing spring' I take to mean 'the source (of passion) that overwhelms reason'.

2. *thing*] being, creature (drinks); probably derogative (*O.E.D.*, sb.1.10b).

3–4.] The subject of 'Affords' is 'Black choler'; it produces a melancholy passion of ceaseless complaint in the minds of those rejected by their mistresses ('saints').

7. *rage*] inspiration.

9. *Phocion's blushes*] Phocion was an Athenian general and statesman celebrated for his rectitude and hatred of flattery. Burton, 'Democritus to the Reader', p. 64, writes of Phocion's scorn of the opinion of the multitude.

10. *what . . . disease?*] What is troubling you?

11–12.] These elliptical expressions are difficult. I interpret, 'The praise of the judicious? Servile smiles? The pleasure you derive from your labours? Your judgement is clouded by suspicion.'

14. *Jealousy*] mistrust of self and others' praise.

15. *Humfrey Howorth*] was admitted to the Middle Temple 18 June 1624.

Of the Lover's Melancholy.

'Tis not the language, nor the fore-placed rhymes
Of friends, that shall commend to after-times
The Lover's Melancholy: its own worth,
Without a borrowed praise, shall set it forth.
                                                    'Ο φίλos.   5

---

5. 'Ο φίλos] the friend.

THE PROLOGUE

To tell ye, gentlemen, in what true sense
The writer, actors, or the audience
Should mould their judgements for a play, might draw
Truth into rules, but we have no such law.
Our writer, for himself, would have ye know 5
That in his following scenes he doth not owe
To others' fancies; nor hath lain in wait
For any stolen invention from whose height
He might commend his own, more than the right
A scholar claims may warrant for delight. 10
It is arts' scorn that some of late have made
The noble use of poetry a trade.
For your parts, gentlemen, to quit his pains,
Yet you will please that, as you meet with strains
Of lighter mixtures, but to cast your eye 15
Rather upon the main than on the bye.
His hopes stand firm, and we shall find it true,
The Lover's Melancholy cured by you.

6–10.] Ford disclaims plagiarism except what a scholar may justifiably borrow for the pleasure of his readers. See Introduction, pp. 3–10.
11. *arts'*] or art's. Q reads *Arts*.
13. *quit his pains*] reward his labours.
16. *bye*] subsidiary.

DRAMATIS PERSONAE

PALADOR, *Prince of Cyprus.*
AMETHUS, *cousin to the Prince.*
MELEANDER, *formerly statesman to the Prince's father.*
SOPHRONOS, *brother of Meleander and counsellor to the Prince.*
MENAPHON, *son of Sophronos.*
ARETUS, *tutor to the Prince.*
CORAX, *a physician.*
RHETIAS, *a follower of Meleander and protector of Eroclea.*
PELIAS,
CUCULUS, } *foolish courtiers.*
TROLLIO, *servant to Meleander.*
GRILLA, *page to Cuculus.*
THAMASTA, *sister of Amethus.*
EROCLEA [Parthenophill],
CLEOPHILA, } *daughters of Meleander.*
KALA, *maid to Thamasta.*

DRAMATIS PERSONAE] *Weber subst.*

The Lover's Melancholy

Act I Scene i

Enter MENAPHON *and* PELIAS.

Menaphon. Dangers! How mean you dangers, that so courtly
   You gratulate my safe return from dangers?
Pelias. From travels, noble sir.
Menaphon.   These are delights,
   If my experience hath not truant-like
   Misspent the time, which I have strove to use   5
   For bettering my mind with observation.
Pelias. As I am modest, I protest 'tis strange;
   But is it possible?
Menaphon.   What?
Pelias.   To bestride
   The frothy foams of Neptune's surging waves
   When blust'ring Boreas tosseth up the deep   10
   And thumps a thunder bounce?
Menaphon.   Sweet sir, 'tis nothing.
   Straight comes a dolphin playing near your ship,
   Heaving his crooked back up, and presents
   A feather-bed to waft 'ee to the shore
   As easily as if you slept i'th' court.   15
Pelias. Indeed, is't true, I pray?
Menaphon.   I will not stretch
   Your faith upon the tenters; prithee, Pelias,

Act I] Actus I. Scena I. Q.

---

   2. *gratulate*] congratulate.
   10. *Boreas*] the north wind, worshipped as a deity by the Greeks.
   11. *bounce*] resounding thump. O.E.D. (sb.1.1) quotes this example.
   12–15.] Pliny, *Natural History*, IX.viii–x, describes the supposed tameness and intelligence of the dolphin, including its willingness to carry humans on its back. Cf. *Tw.N.*, I.i.15, 'Arion on the dolphin's back'.
   14. *'ee*] ye; a characteristic form throughout Q.
   17. *tenters*] A tenter was a wooden framework used for stretching and drying in the manufacture of cloth.

Where didst thou learn this language?
Pelias.   I this language?
Alas, sir, we that study words and forms
Of compliment must fashion all discourse   20
According to the nature of the subject.
But I am silent; now appears a sun
Whose shadow I adore.

Enter AMETHUS, SOPHRONOS, *and* Attendants.

Menaphon.   My honoured father!
Sophronos. From mine eyes, son, son of my care, my love,
The joys that bid thee welcome do too much   25
   Speak me a child.
Menaphon.   O princely sir, your hand.
Amethus. Perform your duties where you owe them first;
I dare not be so sudden in the pleasures
Thy presence hath brought home.
Sophronos.   Here thou still find'st
A friend as noble, Menaphon, as when   30
Thou left'st at thy departure.
Menaphon.   Yes, I know it;
To him I owe more service——
Amethus.   Pray give leave.
[*To Sophronos.*] He shall attend your entertainments
   soon,
Next day, and next day; for an hour or two
I would engross him only.
Sophronos.   Noble lord!   35
Amethus. Y'are both dismissed.
Pelias.   Your creature and your servant.

Exeunt all but AMETHUS, MENAPHON.

Amethus. Give me thy hand. I will not say, 'Th'art welcome';
That is the common road of common friends.
I am glad I have thee here——O, I want words

23.1.] *Q prints in right-hand margin to ll. 21–3.*   33. To Sophronos] *This ed.*

    22–3. *now . . . adore*] a nonsensical 'compliment' since the sun does not make a shadow of itself.
    24–6. *From . . . child*] He weeps tears of joy like a child.
    35. *engross*] monopolise.
    36. *Your creature*] one entirely devoted to you. Cf. note to II.i.230.

SC I] THE LOVER'S MELANCHOLY 55

    To let thee know my heart.
Menaphon.   'Tis pieced to mine.   40
Amethus. Yes, 'tis; as firmly as that holy thing
    Called friendship can unite it. Menaphon,
    My Menaphon, now all the goodly blessings
    That can create a heaven on earth dwell with thee!
    Twelve months have we been sundered but, henceforth,   45
    We never more will part till that sad hour
    In which death leaves the one of us behind
    To see the other's funerals performed.
    Let's now a while be free. How have thy travels
    Disburthened thee abroad of discontents?   50
Menaphon. Such cure as sick men find in changing beds
    I found in change of airs; the fancy flattered
    My hopes with ease, as theirs do, but the grief
    Is still the same.
Amethus.   Such is my case at home.
    Cleophila, thy kinswoman, that maid   55
    Of sweetness and humility, more pities
    Her father's poor afflictions than the tide
    Of my complaints.
Menaphon.   Thamasta, my great mistress,
    Your princely sister, hath, I hope ere this,
    Confirmed affection on some worthy choice.   60
Amethus. Not any, Menaphon. Her bosom yet
    Is intermured with ice, though by the truth
    Of love, no day hath ever passed wherein
    I have not mentioned thy deserts, thy constancy,
    Thy——Come, in troth I dare not tell thee what,   65
    Lest thou mightst think I fawned upon a sin
    Friendship was never guilty of; for flattery
    Is monstrous in a true friend.
Menaphon.   Does the court
    Wear the old looks too?
Amethus.   If thou mean'st the prince,

---

  40. *pieced*] joined.
  49. *free*] frank, unrestrained.
  58. *complaints*] lover's entreaties.
  62. *intermured*] walled in.
  66. *fawned upon*] showed a servile fondness for (flattery). The sentiments and tone suggest an echo of *Ham.*, III.ii.54ff.

It does. He's the same melancholy man 70
He was at's father's death; sometimes speaks sense,
But seldom mirth; will smile, but seldom laugh;
Will lend an ear to business, deal in none;
Gaze upon revels, antic fopperies,
But is not moved; will sparingly discourse, 75
Hear music; but what most he takes delight in
Are handsome pictures. One so young and goodly,
So sweet in his own nature, any story
Hath seldom mentioned.
Menaphon.   Why should such as I am
Groan under the light burthens of small sorrows, 80
When as a prince, so potent, cannot shun
Motions of passion? To be man, my lord,
Is to be but the exercise of cares
In several shapes; as miseries do grow,
They alter as men's forms, but how none know. 85
Amethus. This little isle of Cyprus sure abounds
In greater wonders, both for change and fortune,
Than any you have seen abroad.
Menaphon.   Than any
I have observed abroad; all countries else
To a free eye and mind yield something rare, 90
And I, for my part, have brought home one jewel
Of admirable value.
Amethus.   Jewel, Menaphon?
Menaphon. A jewel, my Amethus, a fair youth;
A youth, whom if I were but superstitious,
I should repute an excellence more high 95
Than mere creations are; to add delight

96–7.] are; to add delight / I'll *So Weber;* are, to adde delight. / I'le *Q.*

   74. *antic fopperies*] grotesque and absurd entertainments. A prefiguring of the Masque of Melancholy (III.iii) which will, indeed, 'move' the prince.
   76–7. *but . . . pictures*] This specific possibly takes its origin in Charles I's connoisseurship in painting. There is, of course, no parallel although the portrayal of Palador is ultimately very flattering.
   82. *motions*] agitations.
   84. *several*] various.
   89. *else*] on any other supposition (*O.E.D.*, 4), i.e. than 'change and fortune' (l. 87).
   94–6.] If he believed in the supernatural Menaphon would have reckoned the youth to be a god; 'mere creations': mortal beings.

SC I]   THE LOVER'S MELANCHOLY   57

  I'll tell ye how I found him.
Amethus.   Prithee do.
Menaphon. Passing from Italy to Greece, the tales
 Which poets of an elder time have feigned
 To glorify their Tempe bred in me   100
 Desire of visiting that paradise.
 To Thessaly I came, and living private,
 Without acquaintance of more sweet companions
 Than the old inmates to my love, my thoughts,
 I day by day frequented silent groves   105
 And solitary walks. One morning early
 This accident encountered me: I heard
 The sweetest and most ravishing contention
 That art or nature ever were at strife in.
Amethus. I cannot yet conceive what you infer 110
 By art and nature.
Menaphon.   I shall soon resolve ye.
 A sound of music touched mine ears, or rather,
 Indeed, entranced my soul. As I stole nearer,
 Invited by the melody, I saw
 This youth, this fair-faced youth, upon his lute, 115
 With strains of strange variety and harmony,
 Proclaiming, as it seemed, so bold a challenge
 To the clear quiristers of the woods, the birds,
 That as they flocked about him all stood silent,
 Wondering at what they heard. I wondered too. 120
Amethus. And so do I, good——on!
Menaphon.   A nightingale,

106–9.] *Q has marginal note: Vide Fami. | stradam. Lib. 2. | Prolus. 6. Acad. | 2. Imitat. | Clau- | dian.*

---

 99. *feigned*] imagined. Cf. *A.Y.L.*, III.iii.16–17, 'the truest poetry is the most feigning'.
 100. *Tempe*] valley in Thessaly, between Mount Olympus at the north and Ossa at the south, celebrated by ancient poets for its beauty and temperate climate.
 102. *Thessaly*] north-east sector of Greece; its chief river, the Peneus, flowed into the Aegean through the vale of Tempe.
 106–9.] For the marginal note Ford supplied at these lines, '*Vide Fami. stradam. lib. 2. Prolus. 6. Acad. 2. Imitat. Claudian*', see Introduction, pp. 4–5, and Appendix A.
 111. *resolve ye*] clear your doubt.
 118. *quiristers*] choristers.
 121. *good*] common absolute vocative usage; good man, friend etc.

>   Nature's best skilled musician, undertakes
>   The challenge, and for every several strain
>   The well-shaped youth could touch she sung her down;
>   He could not run division with more art   125
>   Upon his quaking instrument than she,
>   The nightingale, did with her various notes
>   Reply to; for a voice and for a sound,
>   Amethus, 'tis much easier to believe
>   That such they were than hope to hear again.   130
> *Amethus.* How did the rivals part?
> *Menaphon.*   You term them rightly;
>   For they were rivals, and their mistress, harmony.
>   Some time thus spent, the young man grew at last
>   Into a pretty anger that a bird
>   Whom art had never taught clefs, moods, or notes,   135
>   Should vie with him for mastery, whose study
>   Had busied many hours to perfect practice.
>   To end the controversy, in a rapture
>   Upon his instrument he plays so swiftly,
>   So many voluntaries, and so quick,   140
>   That there was curiosity and cunning,
>   Concord in discord, lines of differing method
>   Meeting in one full centre of delight.
> *Amethus.* Now for the bird.
> *Menaphon.*   The bird, ordained to be
>   Music's first martyr, strove to imitate   145

124. down] *Q;* own *Gifford.*

---

123. *several strain*] different melody. 'Strain' may possibly have a more precise significance, i.e. 'section' or 'stanza' of music (*O.E.D.*, sb.2.III.11). This sense would link with 'down' in the next line.

124. *down*] refrain, chorus (*O.E.D.*, sb.3.I). Gifford and subsequent editors unnecessarily emend to 'own'.

125. *division*] a rapid melodic passage, especially as a variation on, or accompaniment to, a theme. Hence 'run division': to execute such a passage.

135. *clefs*] characters in musical notation which indicate the pitch of the music.

moods] Mood is probably used here in its reference to time values in music, but it could have the more general sense of 'mode', 'tone' (*O.E.D.*, sb.2.3a, 3c).

140. *voluntaries*] spontaneous passages.

141. *curiosity and cunning*] ingenuity and skill.

143. *centre*] concentration.

These several sounds; which, when her warbling throat
Failed in, for grief down dropped she on his lute
And brake her heart. It was the quaintest sadness
To see the conqueror upon her hearse
To weep a funeral elegy of tears, 150
That trust me, my Amethus, I could chide
Mine own unmanly weakness that made me
A fellow-mourner with him.
Amethus.   I believe thee.
Menaphon. He looks upon the trophies of his art,
Then sighed, then wiped his eyes, then sighed, and cried, 155
'Alas, poor creature! I will soon revenge
This cruelty upon the author of it.
Henceforth this lute, guilty of innocent blood,
Shall never more betray a harmless peace
To an untimely end.' And in that sorrow, 160
As he was pashing it against a tree,
I suddenly stepped in.
Amethus.   Thou hast discoursed
A truth of mirth and pity.
Menaphon.   I reprieved
Th'intended execution with entreaties
And interruption. But, my princely friend, 165
It was not strange the music of his hand
Did over-match birds, when his voice and beauty,
Youth, carriage, and discretion, must from men
Endued with reason ravish admiration;
From me they did.
Amethus.   But is this miracle 170
Not to be seen?
Menaphon.   I won him by degrees
To choose me his companion. Whence he is,
Or who, as I durst modestly enquire,
So gently he would woo not to make known;
Only, for reasons to himself reserved, 175
He told me that some remnant of his life

---

154. looks] *Q;* look'd *Weber.*

---

160. *Untimely*] premature.
161. *pashing*] dashing.
174. *woo*] entreat.

    Was to be spent in travel; for his fortunes,
    They were nor mean nor riotous; his friends
    Not published to the world, though not obscure;
    His country, Athens, and his name, Parthenophill.   180
Amethus. Came he with you to Cyprus?
Menaphon.   Willingly.
    The fame of our young melancholy prince,
    Meleander's rare distractions, the obedience
    Of young Cleophila, Thamasta's glory,
    Your matchless friendship, and my desperate love,   185
    Prevailed with him, and I have lodged him privately
    In Famagosta.
Amethus.   Now th'art doubly welcome;
    I will not lose the sight of such a rarity
    For one part of my hopes. When d'ee intend
    To visit my great-spirited sister?
Menaphon.   May I   190
    Without offence?
Amethus.   Without offence! Parthenophill
    Shall find a worthy entertainment too.
    Thou art not still a coward?
Menaphon.   She's too excellent,
    And I too low in merit.
Amethus.   I'll prepare
    A noble welcome; and, friend, ere we part,   195
    Unload to thee an over-chargèd heart.   *Exeunt.*

Act I   Scene ii

Enter RHETIAS, *carelessly attired.*

Rhetias. I will not court the madness of the times,
    Nor fawn upon the riots that embalm

    177–8. *his . . . riotous*] He was neither poor nor so rich as to afford a lavish style of life.
    179. *Not . . . world*] not publicly known.
    183. *rare distractions*] strange mental disorders.
    189. *For . . . hopes*] Taking 'for' to mean 'as being' (Abbott, 148), I interpret 'as representing one part of what I hope to enjoy'. The other part is Menaphon; he is doubly welcome, for himself and for Parthenophill. E. A. J. Honigmann suggests 'in exchange for a (substantial) part of what I hope to have (as my future fortune)'.
    1–22.] The stance of 'Be mine own antic' (l. 13) is reminiscent of Marston's *Malcontent* and *Antonio* plays, and so are the Stoic sentiments, but the latter reiterate traditional moral ideas in Ford's *Line of Life* and *Golden Mean*.

SC II]   THE LOVER'S MELANCHOLY   61

  Our wanton gentry to preserve the dust
  Of their affected vanities in coffins
  Of memorable shame. When commonwealths   5
  Totter and reel from that nobility
  And ancient virtue which renowns the great,
  Who steer the helm of government, while mushrooms
  Grow up and make new laws to licence folly,
  Why should not I, a May-game, scorn the weight 10
  Of my sunk fortunes? Snarl at the vices
  Which rot the land, and without fear or wit
  Be mine own antic? 'Tis a sport to live
  When life is irksome, if we will not hug
  Prosperity in others and contemn   15
  Affliction in ourselves. This rule is certain:
  He that pursues his safety from the school
  Of state, must learn to be madman or fool.
  Ambition, wealth, ease, I renounce—the devil
  That damns ye here on earth. Or I will be—— 20
  Mine own mirth, or mine own tormentor——So!

Enter PELIAS.

  Here comes intelligence, a buzz o' the court.
Pelias. Rhetias, I sought thee out to tell thee news,
  New, excellent new news. Cuculus, sirrah,

19. renounce—the] *Gifford;* renounce the Q.

Strength of conviction on Ford's part seems to override strict relevance to Palador's on the whole exemplary court.
 7. *renowns*] makes famous.
 8. *mushrooms*] upstarts.
 10. *May-game*] laughing-stock. The term derives from May Day amusements.
 12. *wit*] discretion. Rhetias is careless of the consequences of his actions.
 13. *antic*] buffoon.
 14. *hug*] value.
 17–18.] 'From' can hardly mean 'away from' (Abbott, §158) since outside the milieu of statecraft one would presumably be out of danger and not have to act as fool or madman; either, 'He that seeks his safety out of the study of statecraft must learn to be a madman or a fool'; or, possibly, 'He that seeks to be safe from (the perils of) statecraft must learn to be a madman or a fool'. Each of these lines begins with double inverted commas in Q to indicate a *sententia.*
 21. *Mine own mirth*] object of amusement to myself.
 22. *intelligence*] news.
 a buzz] a busy rumour (*O.E.D.*, sb.1.3.b).

That gull, that young old gull, is coming this way. 25
Rhetias. And thou art his forerunner?
Pelias.   Prithee, hear me.
Instead of a fine guarded page we have got him
A boy, tricked up in neat and handsome fashion,
Persuaded him that 'tis indeed a wench,
And he has entertained him. He does follow him, 30
Carries his sword and buckler, waits on his trencher,
Fills him his wine, tobacco, whets his knife,
Lackeys his letters, does what service else
He would employ his man in. Being asked
Why he is so irregular in courtship, 35
His answer is, that since great ladies use
Gentlemen ushers to go bare before them,
He knows no reason but he may reduce
The courtiers to have women wait on them,
And he begins the fashion. He is laughed at 40
Most complimentally. Thou'lt burst to see him.
Rhetias. Agelastus, so surnamed for his gravity, was a very
wise fellow, kept his countenance all days of his life as
demurely as a judge that pronounceth sentence of death
on a poor rogue for stealing as much bacon as would serve 45

27–8.] *Weber; four lines in Q* . . . Page, / . . . him ╱ . . handsome / Fashion; 42–7.] *Prose Weber; verse in Q* . . . grauity, / . . . countenance / . . . that / . . . Roague, / . . . meale / . . . . once, / . . . Scholler?

---

26. *forerunner*] herald to a great man. Heavily sarcastic – Pelias is less than the simpleton (gull) he heralds.
27. *guarded*] wearing a richly trimmed livery.
30. *he . . . him*] he has taken him into his service.
31. *buckler*] small round shield.
trencher] plate or platter, often wooden.
33. *lackeys*] attends to.
35. *courtship*] court etiquette.
37. *bare*] bare-headed; a token of respect.
41. *complimentally*] courteously.
42–50. *Agelastus . . . thistles*] Agelastus, 'the unsmiling', a name given to Marcus Crassus, grandfather of the triumvir Marcus Licinius Crassus (Cicero, *De Finibus*, V.xxx.92). The episode of ass and thistles, deriving from the Roman satirist Lucilius, is related by St Jerome (*Letter* 7). The point of the jibe is that Pelias shows the asinine level of his own taste and wit in finding such foolery entertaining. The basic idea, 'like lips, like lettuce', is found in other plays of the period, e.g. Massinger's *The Guardian*, II.iii.37–8, Dekker and Webster's *Westward Ho*, II.ii.191 (*Dramatic Works of Thomas Dekker*, ed. Fredson Bowers (Cambridge, 1955), vol. II).

at a meal with a calf's head. Yet he smiled once, and never
but once. Thou art no scholar?
Pelias. I have read pamphlets dedicated to me.
Dost call him Agelastus? Why did he laugh?
Rhetias. To see an ass eat thistles. Puppy, go study to be a 50
singular coxcomb. Cuculus is an ordinary ape, but thou
art an ape of an ape.
Pelias. Thou hast a patent to abuse thy friends.
Look, look, he comes! Observe him seriously.

Enter CUCULUS *and* GRILLA.

Cuculus. Reach me my sword and buckler. 55
Grilla. They are here, forsooth.
Cuculus. How now, minx, how now! Where is your duty, your
distance? Let me have service methodically tendered; you
are now one of us. Your curtsey. [*Grilla curtsies.*] Good;
remember that you are to practise courtship. Was thy 60
father a piper, say'st thou?
Grilla. A sounder of some such wind instrument, forsooth.
Cuculus. Was he so? Hold up thy head. Be thou musical to me
and I will marry thee to a dancer; one that shall ride on his
footcloth, and maintain thee in thy muff and hood. 65
Grilla. That will be find indeed.
Cuculus. Thou art yet but simple.

54.1.] As Dyce; after l. 52 Q.   59. Grilla curtsies] So Weber.   63–5.] *Prose
Weber; Q lineation indicates prose/verse confusion.*

---

53. *patent*] letters patent, licence. Although Rhetias is not a fully developed
malcontent he is here accorded the measure of freedom allowed to the role to
be blunt and satirical.

62.] Grilla's answer implies that her father was a sow-gelder since the sow-gelder used to blow a horn. Burton (p. 687; 3: 2: 2: 3) refers mockingly to the sow-gelder and his horn as being an appropriate herald for a wanton and gaudily dressed woman; this may have suggested the parentage of the fantastically dressed Grilla. But perhaps Ford only intended a crude pun on 'wind instrument'.

64. *dancer*] dancing master (*O.E.D.*, 1.b). The idea is suggested by Grilla's 'musical' father and coarsened further by the sexual connotation of 'dancing' (Partridge, p. 91). Cf. *Chaste Maid in Cheapside*, I.i.15, ed. R. B. Parker (London, 1969).

65. *footcloth*] richly ornamented cloth laid over the back of a horse, reaching to the ground on either side.

muff and hood] The muff, an expensive accessory at the time, was still in fashion in the early seventeenth century, but the hood was no longer being

Grilla. D'ee think so?
Cuculus. I have a brain, I have a head-piece. O' my conscience, if I take pains with thee, I should raise thy understanding, girl, to the height of a nurse, or a court-midwife at least; I will make thee big in time, wench. 70
Grilla. Even do your pleasure with me, sir.
Pelias. [*Coming forward.*] Noble, accomplished Cuculus!
Rhetias. [*Coming forward.*] Give me thy fist, innocent. 75
Cuculus. Would 'twere in thy belly! There 'tis.
Pelias. That's well; he's an honest blade, though he be blunt.
Cuculus. Who cares? We can be as blunt as he, for's life.
Rhetias. Cuculus, there is within a mile or two a sow-pig hath sucked a brach, and now hunts the deer, the hare, nay, most unnaturally, the wild boar, as well as any hound in Cyprus. 80
Cuculus. Monstrous sow-pig! Is't true?
Pelias. I'll be at charge of a banquet on thee for a sight of her.
Rhetias. Everything takes after the dam that gave it suck. Where hadst thou thy milk? 85
Cuculus. I? Why, my nurse's husband was a most excellent maker of shuttle-cocks.
Pelias. My nurse was a woman-surgeon.
Rhetias. And who gave thee pap, mouse? 90
Grilla. I never sucked that I remember.
Rhetias. La, now, a shuttle-cock maker! All thy brains are stuck with cork and feather, Cuculus. This learned courtier takes after the nurse too, a she-surgeon, which is, in effect, a mere matcher of colours. Go, learn to paint and 95

74. *Coming forward*] Weber.   75. *Coming forward*] Dyce.

---

worn by court ladies and would have been associated by the audience with citizens' wives (Linthicum, pp. 232–4, 274–5).
69. *head-piece*] See note to II.i.37–8.
70–2. *if ... wench*] bawdy puns; 'understanding', 'big'. Cf. Grilla's reply. The vein is perhaps continued in 'innocent' (l. 75), a natural fool, who by reason of his 'bauble' gives pleasure to ladies.
77. *blade*] good fellow.
blunt] play on literal and figurative senses.
79–82. *Cuculus ... Cyprus*] Burton suggests that melancholy may be transmitted through the nurse's milk and cites: 'A sow-pig by chance sucked a brach, and, when she was grown, would miraculously hunt all manner of deer, and that as well, or rather better than any ordinary hound' (p. 282; 1: 2: 4: 1). 'brach': bitch hound.
84. *I'll ... thee*] I'll treat you to a banquet.
89. *woman-surgeon*] dealer in paints and cosmetics for ladies (Gifford).

daub compliments, 'tis the next step to run into a new suit.
My Lady Periwinkle here never sucked; suck thy master,
and bring forth moon-calves, fop, do. This is good
philosophy, sirs, make use on't.
Grilla. Bless us, what a strange creature this is!   100
Cuculus. A gull, an arrant gull, by proclamation.

           Enter CORAX, *passing over.*

Pelias. Corax, the prince's chief physician. What business
speeds his haste?——Are all things well, sir?
Corax. Yes, yes, yes.
Rhetias. Phew! you may wheel about, man; we know y'are   105
proud of your slovenry and practice; 'tis your virtue. The
prince's melancholy fit, I presume, holds still.
Corax. So do thy knavery and desperate beggary.
Cuculus. Aha! here's one will tickle the ban-dog.
Rhetias. You must not go yet.   110
Corax. I'll stay in spite of thy teeth. There lies my gravity.
  Casts off his gown. Do what thou darest, I stand thee.
Rhetias. Mountebanks, empirics, quacksalvers, mineralists,

113. Mountebanks] *Weber;* Mountebanck *Q.*

---

96. *'tis . . . suit*] the quickest way to acquire a new suit (i.e. by flattery).
97. *Periwinkle*] playful term for a woman (*O.E.D.*, Periwinkle 1.2.b). The two citations for this use are for 1633 and 1640, both from Shirley's plays. Eleventh-century herbals attributed magical and curative powers to the plant and it was also an ingredient of an aphrodisiac.
98. *moon-calves*] misshapen births, monstrosities.
101. *A . . . proclamation*] Rhetias has not, of course, been publicly denounced as a gull; he has proclaimed himself to be so by what his own words manifest.
101.1. *passing over*] 'Passing over the stage' and variants of this direction, often found in plays of the period, are discussed by Allardyce Nicoll, *Shakespeare Survey*, 12, pp. 47–55. Although his argument that such directions intended entry by the yard and then on to the stage has force for processional movements and other special circumstances, the staging here would not necessarily require it.
105. *wheel about*] To the primary sense of 'go around' or 'go up and down' may possibly be added the inference that Corax is giddy-headed, a bit mad (*O.E.D.*, vb.I.1.c).
106. *slovenry*] slovenliness.
  practice] trickery.
109. *ban-dog*] a dog fastened up, either to guard a house or on account of its ferocity.
111. *There . . . gravity*] He casts off with his gown his status as dignified scholar to exchange abuse with Rhetias. The action recalls *Tp.*, I.ii.25, 'Lie there my art'.
113–15. *Mountebanks . . . barbers*] Cf. Burton: 'Now for Physicians, there

66   THE LOVER'S MELANCHOLY   [ACT I

  wizards, alchemists, cast-apothecaries, old wives, and
  barbers, are all suppositors to the right worshipful doctor,   115
  as I take it. Some of ye are the head of your art—and the
  horns too, but they come by nature. Thou livest single for
  no other end, but that thou fearest to be a cuckold.
Corax. Have at thee! Thou affect'st railing only for thy health;
  thy miseries are so thick and so lasting that thou hast not   120
  one poor denier to bestow on opening a vein. Wherefore,
  to avoid a pleurisy, thou'lt be sure to prate thyself once a
  month into a whipping, and bleed in the breech instead of
  the arm.
Rhetias. Have at thee again!   125
Corax. Come!
Cuculus. There, there, there! O brave doctor!
Pelias. Let 'em alone.
Rhetias. Thou art in thy religion an atheist, in thy condition a
  cur, in thy diet an epicure, in thy lust a goat, in thy sleep a   130
  hog; thou tak'st upon thee the habit of a grave physician,
  but art indeed an imposterous empiric. Physicians are the
  body's cobblers, rather the botchers of men's bodies; as
  the one patches our tattered clothes, so the other solders

133. *body's*] bodies Q; *Gifford omits.*

---

are in every village so many Mountebanks, Empiricks, Quacksalvers, Paracelsians ... Wizards, Alchemists, poor Vicars, cast Apothecaries, Physicians' men, Barbers, and Goodwives' (p. 267; 1: 2: 3: 15).
 Mountebanks] itinerant quacks who proclaimed their medicines from some sort of platform. Their quackery is well imitated in Jonson's *Volpone*, II.ii.
 empirics] medical quacks. The term ultimately derives from Empirici, a sect among ancient physicians and so called because they based their practice on experience and not on philosophical theory (*O.E.D.*, B.sb.1).
 quacksalvers] similar in sense to empirics but with particular reference to supposedly marvellous ointments.
 mineralists] followers of Paracelsus in the use of minerals in medicines; Paracelsus (1493–1541) was a renowned Swiss doctor who held a chair of physic and surgery at Basel. Burton writes of Paracelsus and the use of minerals (pp. 569–70; 2: 4: 1: 4).
 cast] discarded.
 barbers] Barbers also practised surgery and dentistry.
115. *suppositors*] used to induce purgation; pun on 'support'.
121. *denier*] copper coin worth less than a farthing.
122. *avoid*] cure (i.e. by bleeding).
129. *condition*] nature, disposition; could also refer to social status.
132. *imposterous*] having the character of an imposter.
133. *botchers*] tailors who patch clothes.

SC II]   THE LOVER'S MELANCHOLY   67

our diseased flesh. Come on.   135
Cuculus. To't, to't, hold him to't! Hold him to't! To't, to't,
  to't!
Corax. The best worth in thee is the corruption of thy mind,
  for that only entitles thee to the dignity of a louse, a thing
  bred out of the filth and superfluity of ill humours. Thou   140
  bit'st anywhere, and any man who defends not himself
  with the clean linen of secure honesty; him thou darest not
  come near. Thou art fortune's idiot, virtue's bankrupt,
  time's dunghill, manhood's scandal, and thine own
  scourge. Thou wouldst hang thyself so wretchedly mis-   145
  erable thou art, but that no man will trust thee with as
  much money as will buy a halter; and all thy stock to be
  sold is not worth half as much as may procure it.
Rhetias. Ha, ha, ha! This is flattery, gross flattery.
Corax. I have employment for thee, and for ye all. Tut, these   150
  are but good-morrows between us.
Rhetias. Are thy bottles full?
Corax. Of rich wine; let's all suck together.
Rhetias. Like so many swine in a trough.
Corax. I'll shape ye all for a device before the prince; we'll try   155
  how that can move him.
Rhetias. He shall fret or laugh.
Cuculus. Must I make one?
Corax. Yes, and your feminine page too.
Grilla. Thanks, most egregiously.   160
Pelias. I will not slack my part.
Cuculus. Wench, take my buckler.
Corax. Come all unto my chamber; the project is cast; the time

---

133–5.] Cf. Burton: 'Cambyses, in Xenophon, told Cyrus, that to his thinking Physicians were like Tailors and Cobblers, the one mended our sick bodies, as the other did our clothes' (p. 561; 2: 4: 1: 1).

138–40. *The . . . humours*] The general sense is clear although the logic is not. If lice breed in corruption and Rhetias breeds them from the corruption of his mind then he cannot himself be a louse. On 'ill humours' see notes to III.i.103–18.

139. *only*] alone.

152.] presumably a jesting reference to the doctor's urine bottles and meaning, 'Have you had enough?'

155. *shape . . . device*] direct you all for an entertainment.

158. *make one*] be included.

163. *cast*] planned.

only we must attend.
Rhetias. The melody must agree well and yield sport, 165
When such as these are, knaves and fools, consort.
                                            Exeunt.

Act I Scene iii

Enter AMETHUS, THAMASTA, *and* KALA.

Amethus. Does this show well?
Thamasta.   What would you have me do?
Amethus. Not like a lady of the trim, new crept
   Out of the shell of sluttish sweat and labour
   Into the glittering pomp of ease and wantonness,
   Embroideries, and all these antic fashions 5
   That shape a woman monstrous; to transform
   Your education and a noble birth
   Into contempt and laughter. Sister, sister,
   She who derives her blood from princes ought
   To glorify her greatness by humility. 10
Thamasta. Then you conclude me proud?
Amethus.   Young Menaphon,
   My worthy friend, has loved you long and truly;
   To witness his obedience to your scorn
   Twelve months, wronged gentleman, he undertook
   A voluntary exile. Wherefore, sister, 15
   In this time of his absence have you not
   Disposed of your affections on some monarch,
   Or sent ambassadors to some neighb'ring king
   With fawning protestations of your graces,
   Your rare perfections, admirable beauty? 20
   This had been a new piece of modesty
   Would have deserved a chronicle.
Thamasta.   You are bitter;
   And, brother, by your leave, not kindly wise.

165–6.] Rhetias develops a musical metaphor from the suggestion of 'time' in the previous line.

2. *of the trim*] dressed modishly; the following lines suggest the vulgar ostentation of the nouveau riche.

23. *kindly*] according to kin; Amethus, in trying to impose his will upon Thamasta, has a wrong conception of the brother–sister relationship. It turns out that Amethus was justified in urging the suit of Menaphon but the imposition of a brother's will in marriage choice has tragic consequences for Ithocles and Penthea in *The Broken Heart*.

My freedom is my birth's; I am not bound
To fancy your approvements but my own.   25
Indeed, you are an humble youth! I hear of
Your visits and your loving commendation
To your heart's saint, Cleophila, a virgin
Of a rare excellence. What though she want
A portion to maintain a portly greatness?   30
Yet 'tis your gracious sweetness to descend
So low—the meekness of your pity leads ye!
She is your dear friend's sister, a good soul,
An innocent—

Amethus.   Thamasta!
Thamasta.   I have given
Your Menaphon a welcome home as fits me;   35
For his sake entertained Parthenophill,
The handsome stranger, more familiarly
Than, I may fear, becomes me; yet, for his part,
I not repent my courtesies, but you——

Amethus. No more, no more. Be affable to both;   40
Time may reclaim your cruelty.

Thamasta.   I pity
The youth; and trust me, brother, love his sadness.
He talks the prettiest stories; he delivers
His tales so gracefully that I could sit
And listen, nay, forget my meals and sleep 45
To hear his neat discourses. Menaphon
Was well advised in choosing such a friend
For pleading his true love.

Amethus.   Now I commend thee;
Thou'lt change at last I hope.

Thamasta. [*Aside.*]   I fear I shall.

Enter MENAPHON *and* EROCLEA *in man's attire.*

49. *Aside*] Gifford.   49.1.] Dyce subst.; after hope *l*. 49 Q.

29–32. *What ... ye*] Thamasta's sarcasm gets its deserts when she subsequently descends to Parthenophill; 'portly': stately.
   33. *sister*] Cleophila is the cousin, not sister, of Menaphon.
   34. *innocent*] simple creature; a further slight is intended in the common signification 'idiot'.
   39. *I not repent*] For the omission of 'do' before 'not' see Abbott, §305.
   42. *sadness*] seriousness.
   46. *neat*] well expressed.

Amethus. Have ye surveyed the garden?
Menaphon.   'Tis a curious,   50
   A pleasantly contrived delight.
Thamasta.   Your eye, sir,
   Hath in your travels often met contents
   Of more variety.
Eroclea.   Not any, lady.
Menaphon. It were impossible, since your fair presence
   Makes every place where it vouchsafes to shine   55
   More lovely than all other helps of art
   Can equal.
Thamasta.   What you mean by 'helps of art'
   You know yourself best; be they as they are,
   You need none, I am sure, to set me forth.
Menaphon. 'Twould argue want of manners more than skill   60
   Not to praise praise itself.
Thamasta.   For your reward
   Henceforth I'll call you servant.
Amethus.   Excellent sister!
Menaphon. 'Tis my first step to honour. May I fall
   Lower than shame when I neglect all service
   That may confirm this favour.
Thamasta.   Are you well, sir?   65
Eroclea. Great princess, I am well; to see a league
   Between an humble love, such as my friend's is,
   And a commanding virtue, such as yours is,
   Are sure restoratives.
Thamasta.   You speak ingeniously.
   Brother, be pleased to show the gallery   70
   To this young stranger; use the time a while
   And we will all together to the court.
   I will present ye, sir, unto the prince.
Eroclea. Y'are all composed of fairness and true bounty.
Amethus. Come, come. We'll wait thee, sister. This beginning   75
   Doth relish happy process.

---

   52. *contents*] things that give satisfaction, delights.
   59. *set me forth*] praise me.
   62. *servant*] a term in the language of courtly love indicating acceptance of courtship.
   65. *Are . . . sir?*] Eroclea silently betrays her emotions at Thamasta's acceptance of her cousin's courtship. Cf. her reaction to Cleophila's pledge of love to Amethus, II.ii.139–47.
   76. *relish . . . process*] suggests a favourable development.

SC III]   THE LOVER'S MELANCHOLY   71

Menaphon.   You have blessed me.
                   Exeunt all but THAMASTA *and* KALA.
Thamasta. Kala, O Kala!
Kala.   Lady?
Thamasta.   We are private:
   Thou art my closet.
Kala.   Lock your secrets close then;
   I am not to be forced.
Thamasta.   Never till now
   Could I be sensible of being traitor   80
   To honour and to shame.
Kala.   You are in love.
Thamasta. I am grown base——Parthenophill——
Kala.   He's handsome,
   Richly endowed; he hath a lovely face,
   A winning tongue.
Thamasta.   If ever I must fall
   In him my greatness sinks. Love is a tyrant,   85
   Resisted. Whisper in his ear how gladly
   I would steal time to talk with him one hour;
   But do it honourably. Prithee, Kala,
   Do not betray me.
Kala.   Madam, I will make it
   Mine own case; he shall think I am in love with him.   90
Thamasta. I hope thou art not, Kala.
Kala.   'Tis for your sake
   I'll tell him so, but, faith, I am not, lady.
Thamasta. Pray use me kindly; let me not too soon
   Be lost in my new follies. 'Tis a fate
   That overrules our wisdoms; whilst we strive   95
   To live most free we're caught in our own toils.
   Diamonds cut diamonds; they who will prove
   To thrive in cunning, must cure love with love.
                                      Exeunt.

98.1. *Exeunt*] Weber; Exit. | Finis Actus Primi. Q.

   78. *closet*] private repository or cabinet for papers.
   81. *shame*] modesty. Cf. III.ii.92.
   94–5. *'Tis . . . wisdoms*] Falling in love is the overthrow of reason. Proverbial (Tilley, L 517).
   97. *Diamonds . . . diamonds*] proverbial (Tilley, D 323).
   98. *cure . . . love*] a variation of the proverb 'One love drives out another' (Tilley, L 538). She will cure Menaphon's love for her by bestowing hers on Parthenophill. Disastrously, she almost succeeds; cf. III.ii.188ff.

Act II

ACT II SCENE i

Enter SOPHRONOS *and* ARETUS.

Sophronos. Our commonwealth is sick; 'tis more than time
That we should wake the head thereof, who sleeps
In the dull lethargy of lost security.
The commons murmur and the nobles grieve,
The court is now turned antic and grows wild,   5
Whiles all the neighb'ring nations stand at gaze,
And watch fit opportunity to wreak
Their just-conceivèd fury on such injuries
As the late prince, our living master's father,
Committed against laws of truth or honour.   10
Intelligence comes flying in on all sides,
Whilst the unsteady multitude presume
How that you, Aretus, and I, engross
Out of particular ambition
Th'affairs of government—which I, for my part,   15
Groan under and am weary of.
 Aretus.   Sophronos,
I am as zealous too of shaking off
My gay state fetters, that I have bethought

Act II] Actus II. Scena I. Q.   16–17.] of. / *Aret. Sophronos,* / I Q *corr.;* of / *Sophronos.* / *Aret.* I Q *uncorr.*

 1–16.] The condition of the state described here by Sophronos is what in theory would arise under a prince neglectful of his duties but it is not what we actually find in the play where the interest is in psychological not political disorder. The 'antic' behaviour of Cuculus is small evidence of a 'wild' court. The speech is, like Rhetias' soliloquy (I.ii.1–22), consonant with the moral concerns of Ford's prose pamphlets but remains unassimilated to the fabric of the play.

 3. *lost security*] groundless confidence of safety.
 5. *antic*] fantastic.
 14. *particular*] private.

Of speedy remedy; and to that end,
As I have told ye, have concluded with 20
Corax, the prince's chief physician.
Sophronos. You should have done this sooner, Aretus;
You were his tutor and could best discern
His dispositions to inform them rightly.
Aretus. Passions of violent nature by degrees 25
Are easiliest reclaimed. There's something hid
Of his distemper which we'll now find out.

Enter CORAX, RHETIAS, PELIAS, CUCULUS *and* GRILLA.

You come on just appointment. Welcome, gentlemen!
Have you won Rhetias, Corax?
Corax.   Most sincerely.
Cuculus. Save ye, nobilities! Do your lordships take notice of 30
my page? 'Tis a fashion of the newest edition, spick and
span new, without example. Do your honour, housewife.
Grilla. There's a curtsey for you, and a curtsey for you.
Sophronos. 'Tis excellent; we must all follow fashion
And entertain she-waiters.
Aretus.   'Twill be courtly. 35
Cuculus. I think so; I hope the chronicles will rear me one day
for a head-piece——
Rhetias. Of woodcock without brains in't. Barbers shall wear
thee on their citterns, and hucksters set thee out in
gingerbread. 40

34–5.] *Weber; prose in* Q.

---

20. *concluded*] arranged.
23–4. *could . . . rightly*] were the best judge of his mental inclinations and hence able to direct them appropriately.
26–7. *There's . . . distemper*] There's some secret at the back of his mental disorder.
28. *on . . . appointment*] at exactly the appointed moment.
36–7. *rear . . . head-piece*] exalt me as a man of brains. Head-piece could signify the brain itself or the skull which contains it and Rhetias is quick to exploit the double sense in his reply.
38. *woodcock*] proverbially foolish bird.
38–9. *Barbers . . . citterns*] The cittern, a stringed instrument sometimes kept in barbers' shops for the use of customers, was often decorated with a grotesquely carved head. Secco, the barber in *The Fancies*, is abused as 'a cittern-headed gewgaw' (I.ii; vol. II, 234).
39–40. *hucksters . . . gingerbread*] Pedlars will sell gingerbread baked in his shape.

74 THE LOVER'S MELANCHOLY [ACT II

Cuculus. Devil take thee! I say nothing to thee now; canst let
  me be quiet?
Grilla. Y'are too perstreperous, sauce-box.
Cuculus. Good girl! If we begin to puff once—
Pelias. Prithee, hold thy tongue, the lords are in the presence. 45
Rhetias. Mum, butterfly!
Pelias.   O, the prince! Stand and keep silence.
                                                Soft music.
Cuculus. O, the prince! Wench, thou shalt see the prince now.

     Enter PALADOR, *the Prince, with a book in his hand.*

Sophronos.} Sir! gracious sir!
Aretus.
Palador.   Why all this company?
Corax. A book! Is this the early exercise
  I did prescribe? Instead of following health, 50
  Which all men covet, you pursue disease.
  Where's your great horse, your hounds, your set at tennis,
  Your balloon ball, the practice of your dancing,
  Your casting of the sledge, or learning how
  To toss a pike? All changed into a sonnet? 55
  Pray, sir, grant me free liberty to leave
  The court, it does infect me with the sloth
  Of sleep and surfeit. In the university
  I have employments which to my profession

45–6.] *Dyce; prose in* Q.   46.1. *Soft music*] *This ed.; at l.* 47 Q.   51. disease] *Weber;* your disease Q.

41–2. *let . . . quiet*] leave me in peace.
43. *perstreperous*] noisy. A rare word (from Latin 'perstrepere', to make much noise, this example from Ford being the only one cited in *O.E.D.*
44. *If . . . once*] Just let us start showing what we are made of; 'puff': to speak or behave insolently (*O.E.D.*, vb.2).
45. *presence*] presence chamber or ceremonial dais where royalty gave audience.
46. *butterfly*] a term commonly applied to foppish courtiers. Cf. *Lear*, V.iii.13, 'gilded butterflies'.
52–5. *Where's . . . pike*] Sports and pastimes were approved by Elizabethan educationalists for health of body and mind. Burton includes 'balloon' and 'riding of great horses' among his list of sports beneficial for the cure of melancholy (p. 443; 2: 2: 4).
53. *balloon ball*] a game in which an inflated leather ball is struck to and fro by the arms, to which are attached wooden guards.
54. *casting . . . sledge*] throwing the hammer.

SC I]   THE LOVER'S MELANCHOLY   75

> Add profit and report; here I am lost   60
> And in your wilful dulness held a man
> Of neither art nor honesty. You may
> Command my head; pray, take it, do; 'twere better
> For me to lose it than to lose my wits
> And live in bedlam. You will force me to't;   65
> I am almost mad already.

Palador.   I believe it.

Sophronos. Letters are come from Crete which do require
> A speedy restitution of such ships,
> As by your father were long since detained;
> If not, defiance threatened.

Aretus.   These near parts   70
> Of Syria that adjoin muster their friends,
> And by intelligence we learn for certain
> The Syrian will pretend an ancient interest
> Of tribute intermitted.

Sophronos.   Through your land
> Your subjects mutter strangely, and imagine   75
> More than they dare speak publicly.

Corax.   And yet
> They talk but oddly of you.

Cuculus.   Hang 'em, mongrels!

Palador. Of me! My subjects talk of me?

Corax.   Yes, scurvily,
> And think worse, prince.

Palador.   I'll borrow patience
> A little time to listen to these wrongs,   80
> And from the few of you which are here present,
> Conceive the general voice.

Corax. [*Aside.*]   So—now he is nettled.

Palador. By all your loves I charge ye, without fear
> Or flattery, to let me know your thoughts

82. *Aside*] Weber.

---

60. *report*] reputation.
65. *bedlam*] hospital of St Mary of Bethlehem in London, an asylum for the mentally deranged.
70. *defiance*] war.
73–4. *The . . . intermitted*] The Syrian king will lay claim to an ancient right to tribute, the payment of which has been neglected. See Introduction, p. 4.
82. *voice*] opinion.

And how I am interpreted. Speak boldly. 85
Sophronos. For my part, sir, I will be plain and brief.
I think you are of nature mild and easy,
Not willingly provoked, but withal headstrong
In any passion that misleads your judgement.
I think you too indulgent to such motions 90
As spring out of your own affections,
Too old to be reformed, and yet too young
To take fit counsel from yourself of what
Is most amiss.
Palador.   So——Tutor, your conceit?
Aretus. I think you dote—with pardon let me speak it— 95
Too much upon your pleasures, and these pleasures
Are so wrapped up in self-love that you covet
No other change of fortune; would be still
What your birth makes you, but are loath to toil
In such affairs of state as break your sleeps. 100
Corax. I think you would be by the world reputed
A man in every point complete, but are
In manners and effect indeed a child,
A boy, a very boy.
Pelias.   May it please your grace,
I think you do contain within yourself 105
The great elixir, soul, and quintessence
Of all divine perfections; are the glory
Of mankind, and the only strict example
For earthly monarchies to square out their lives by;
Time's miracle, fame's pride; in knowledge, wit, 110
Sweetness, discourse, arms, arts——
Palador.   You are a courtier.
Cuculus. But not of the ancient fashion, an't like your highness. 'Tis I, I that am the credit of the court, noble prince; and if thou wouldst by proclamation or patent create me

---

90–1. *motions . . . affections*] impulses deriving from your own inclinations. In view of what Sophronos has just said in the previous lines 'affections' could carry the sense of 'feelings', or 'passions' (*O.E.D.*, sb.II.3).

94. *conceit*] conception of the matter.

106. *elixir*] in alchemy the preparation which could change base metals into gold ('philosopher's stone'), or the 'elixir of life', an essence supposedly able to prolong life indefinitely.

109. *square out*] regulate.

114. *patent*] Monopolies were granted by letters patent from the monarch.

SC I] THE LOVER'S MELANCHOLY 77

  overseer of all the tailors in thy dominions, then, then the 115
  golden days should appear again; bread should be
  cheaper, fools should have more wit, knaves more honesty, and beggars more money.
Grilla. I think now——
Cuculus. Peace, you squall! 120
Palador. [*To Rhetias.*] You have not spoken yet.
Cuculus. Hang him! He'll nothing but rail.
Grilla. Most abominable; out upon him!
Corax. Away, Cuculus; follow the lords.
Cuculus. Close, page, close. 125

   They all fall back and steal out.
   Manet, PALADOR *and* RHETIAS.

Palador. You are somewhat long a'thinking.
Rhetias. I do not think at all.
Palador. Am I not worthy of your thought?
Rhetias. My pity you are—but not my reprehension.
Palador. Pity? 130
Rhetias. Yes, for I pity such to whom I owe service, who exchange their happiness for a misery.
Palador. Is it a misery to be a prince?
Rhetias. Princes who forget their sovereignty and yield to affected passion are weary of command. You had a 135
 father, sir.
Palador. Your sovereign whiles he lived. But what of him?
Rhetias. Nothing. I only dared to name him; that's all.
Palador. I charge thee by the duty that thou owest us
 Be plain in what thou mean'st to speak; there's something 140
 That we must know; be free, our ears are open.

121. *To Rhetias*] Gifford. 125.2. PALADOR] *Prince* Q. 139–41.] *Weber; prose in* Q.

115–18. *then . . . money*] comic evocation of the Golden Age. Given the probable influence of Shakespeare's last plays (see Introduction, p. 8) perhaps a reminiscence of Gonzalo's ideal commonwealth, *Tp.*, II.i.141 ff.
 120. *squall*] abusive term for a small person.
 124.] That Corax should usher every one out to enable Rhetias to speak his mind privately to the Prince suggests that the two are already conspiring together for his cure. See Introduction, pp. 15–16.
 135. *affected passion*] Cf. II.i.90–1 and note.
 137. *whiles*] common alternative form of 'while'.

Rhetias. O, sir, I had rather hold a wolf by the ears than stroke
   a lion—the greatest danger is the last.
Palador. This is mere trifling——Ha! are all stolen hence?
   We are alone. Thou hast an honest look;   145
   Thou hast a tongue, I hope, that is not oiled
   With flattery; be open. Though 'tis true
   That in my younger days I oft have heard
   Agenor's name, my father, more traduced
   Than I could then observe, yet, I protest,   150
   I never had a friend, a certain friend,
   That would inform me throughly of such errors
   As oftentimes are incident to princes.
Rhetias. All this may be. I have seen a man so curious in
   feeling of the edge of a keen knife that he has cut his   155
   fingers. My flesh is not of proof against the metal I am to
   handle; the one is tenderer than the other.
Palador. I see, then, I must court thee. Take the word
   Of a just prince; for anything thou speak'st
   I have more than a pardon—thanks and love.   160
Rhetias. I will remember you of an old tale that something
   concerns you. Meleander, the great but unfortunate
   statesman, was by your father treated with for a match
   between you and his eldest daughter, the lady Eroclea.
   You were both near of an age. I presume you remember a   165
   contract, and cannot forget her.
Palador. She was a lovely beauty. Prithee, forward.
Rhetias. To court was Eroclea brought; was courted by your

148. younger] *Q corr.;* young *Q uncorr.*

142–3.] To hold a wolf by the ears is proverbial (Tilley, W 603) for a terrible dilemma; to hold or let go is equally dangerous, but Rhetias would rather that than stroke a lion, i.e. meddle with a prince.

150. *Than . . . observe*] Presumably he was too young to take much note of the remarks about his father.

152. *throughly*] thoroughly; common alternative form.

156. *not . . . against*] vulnerable to. 'Of proof' was often used to indicate the impenetrability of armour, and 'metal' suggests that idea here.

158. *court*] win by courteous attentions.

162–6. *Meleander . . . contract*] According to Henry Swinburne, *A Treatise of Spousals* (1686), Section XIV, a private betrothal without witnesses was binding in the eyes of God, but a public betrothal, as is the case here, was binding before law and God so that the 'less noble design' (l. 170) of Agenor was particularly reprehensible. (Swinburne's treatise was written *c.* 1600 and is our chief source of knowledge regarding marriage contracts at the time.)

father, not for Prince Palador, as it followed, but to be
made a prey to some less noble design——with your 170
favour, I have forgot the rest.
Palador. Good, call it back again into thy memory,
Else, losing the remainder, I am lost too.
Rhetias. You charm me. In brief, a rape by some bad agents
was attempted; by the lord Meleander her father rescued, 175
she conveyed away, Meleander accused of treason, his
land seized, he himself distracted, and confined to the
castle where he yet lives. What had ensued was doubtful;
but your father shortly after died.
Palador. But what became of fair Eroclea? 180
Rhetias. She never since was heard of.
Palador.   No hope lives then
Of ever, ever seeing her again?
Rhetias. Sir, I feared I should anger ye. There was, as I said,
an old tale; I have now a new one which may perhaps
season the first with a more delightful relish. 185
Palador. I am prepared to hear, say what you please.
Rhetias. My lord Meleander falling, on whose favour my
fortunes relied, I furnished myself for travel and bent my
course to Athens, where a pretty accident after a while
came to my knowledge. 190
Palador. My ear is open to thee.
Rhetias. A young lady contracted to a noble gentleman, as the
lady we last mentioned and your highness were, being
hindered by their jarring parents, stole from her home and
was conveyed like a ship-boy in a merchant from the 195
country where she lived, into Corinth first, and afterwards
to Athens; where in much solitariness she lived like a
youth almost two years, courted by all for acquaintance,
but friend to none by familiarity.
Palador. In habit of a man? 200
Rhetias. A handsome young man; till within these three

183. feared] *Weber;* feare *Q.*

---

174. *charm*] persuade.
rape] abduction.
178. *What ... doubtful*] What might have happened subsequently was uncertain.
185. *relish*] flavour. The metaphor is continued from 'season'.
195. *merchant*] merchant ship.

months or less—her sweetheart's father dying some year
before or more—she had notice of it and with much joy
returned home, and, as report voiced it at Athens, enjoyed
her happiness she was long an exile for. Now, noble sir, if   205
you did love the lady Eroclea why may not such safety and
fate direct her as directed the other? 'Tis not impossible.
Palador. If I did love her, Rhetias. Yes, I did.
  Give me thy hand: as thou didst serve Meleander,
And art still true to these, henceforth serve me.   210
Rhetias. My duty and my obedience are my surety; but I have
been too bold.
Palador. Forget the sadder story of my father
And only, Rhetias, learn to read me well,
For I must thank thee. Th'ast unlocked   215
A tongue was vowed to silence; for requital
Open my bosom, Rhetias.
Rhetias.   What's your meaning?
Palador. To tie thee to an oath of secrecy——
Unloose the buttons, man, thou dost it faintly.
What find'st thou there?
Rhetias.   A picture in a tablet.   220
Palador. Look well upon't.
Rhetias.   I do——yes——let me observe it——
'Tis hers, the lady's.
Palador.   Whose?
Rhetias.   Eroclea's.
Palador. Hers that was once Eroclea. For her sake
Have I advanced Sophronos to the helm
Of government; for her sake will restore   225
Meleander's honours to him; will for her sake
Beg friendship from thee, Rhetias. O, be faithful,
And let no politic lord work from thy bosom
My griefs. I know thou wert put on to sift me;

202. sweetheart's] *Gifford;* sweet hearty *Q.* 205.] happiness . . . for.
Gifford; happinesse: she . . . exile: For *Q.*

---

  210. *these*] these hands.
  214. *read me*] understand my character.
  220. *tablet*] ornament or jewel, flat in shape, usually hung about the neck, and sometimes containing a miniature.
  228. *politic*] crafty; common pejorative use.
  229. *My griefs*] elliptical for 'the nature of (or reason for) my sufferings'.

But be not too secure.
Rhetias. I am your creature. 230
Palador. Continue still thy discontented fashion,
Humour the lords as they would humour me;
I'll not live in thy debt——we are discovered.

Enter AMETHUS, MENAPHON, THAMASTA, KALA, EROCLEA *as before.*

Amethus. Honour and health still wait upon the prince!
Sir, I am bold with favour to present 235
Unto your highness, Menaphon, my friend,
Returned from travel.
Menaphon. Humbly on my knees
I kiss your gracious hand.
Palador. It is our duty
To love the virtuous.
Menaphon. If my prayers or service
Hold any value, they are vowed yours ever. 240
Rhetias. I have a fist for thee too, stripling; th'art started up
prettily since I saw thee. Hast learned any wit abroad?
Canst tell news, and swear lies with a grace, like a true
traveller? What new ouzel's this?
Thamasta. Your highness shall do right to your own
judgement 245
In taking more than common notice of
This stranger, an Athenian named Parthenophill.
One whom, if mine opinion do not soothe me

240. Hold] Hold——Q.

---

230. *be . . . secure*] perhaps continuing the line of thought from 'politic lord', that Rhetias should beware of over-confidence in his ability to keep Palador's secret. Alternatively it may be a mild threat springing from his fears that Rhetias may not be faithful to him. In this case the expanded sense would be, 'Don't be too sure you are safe from my anger (should you betray me).' This interpretation is supported by the reply, 'I am your creature', i.e. entirely devoted to you. 'Creature' was often used, though not here, pejoratively for an unscrupulous tool. Palador's neurotic and groundless fears indicate a mind isolated from the reality of his court.

235. *with favour*] with your favour.

244. *ouzel*] old name for blackbird; Parthenophill's musical contest with the nightingale makes the term curiously appropriate. For its application to a person see *O.E.D.*, 1.c.

248. *whom*] ungrammatical use for the nominative 'who', common then as now.

soothe] flatter.

　　　　　Too grossly, for the fashion of his mind
　　　　　Deserves a dear respect.
Palador.　　　　　　　　Your commendations,　　　　　250
　　　　　Sweet cousin, speak him nobly.
Eroclea.　　　　　　　　All the powers
　　　　　That sentinel just thrones double their guards
　　　　　About your sacred excellence!
Palador.　　　　　　　　What fortune
　　　　　Led him to Cyprus?
Menaphon.　　　　　　My persuasions won him.
Amethus. And if your highness please to hear the entrance　255
　　　　　Into their first acquaintance, you will say——
Thamasta. It was the newest, sweetest, prettiest accident
　　　　　That e'er delighted your attention.
　　　　　I can discourse it, sir.
Palador.　　　　　　　Some other time.
　　　　　How is 'a called?
Thamasta.　　　　　　Parthenophill.
Palador.　　　　　　　　　Parthenophill?　　　　　260
　　　　　We shall sort time to take more notice of him.　　*Exit.*
Menaphon. His wonted melancholy still pursues him.
Amethus. I told you so.
Thamasta.　　　　　　You must not wonder at it.
Eroclea. I do not, lady.
Amethus.　　　　　　　Shall we to the castle?
Menaphon. We will attend ye both.　　　　　　　　265
Rhetias. All three——I'll go too. [*To Amethus.*] Hark in thine
　　ear, gallant: I'll keep the old madman in chat whilst thou
　　gabblest to the girl; my thumb's upon my lips, not a word.
Amethus. [*Aside.*] I need not fear thee, Rhetias——Sister,
　　soon
　　Expect us; this day we will range the city.　　　　　270

251. speak] *Weber;* speakes *Q.*　252. their] *Gifford;* these *Q.*　261. *Exit*] *Exit. Prince Q.*　266. *To Amethus*] *This ed.*　269. *Aside*] *This ed.*

---

260. '*a*] he; familiar form, common in the period, derived from 'ha', a Middle English form of the pronoun.
261. *sort*] find. The sense of 'suitable' is probably included.
265. *We . . . both*] We (Menaphon and Parthenophill) will both attend you.
267–8. *old madman . . . girl*] Meleander . . . Cleophila. Cf. II.ii.126ff. for Rhetias' endeavour to give Amethus opportunity to court Cleophila.
270. *range*] range through.

Thamasta. Well, soon I shall expect ye——[*Aside.*] Kala!
Kala. [*Aside.*] Trust me.
Rhetias. Troop on——Love, love, what a wonder thou art!
Exeunt. KALA *and* EROCLEA *stay.*
Kala. May I not be offensive, sir?
Eroclea. Your pleasure?
Yet pray be brief.
Kala Then briefly, good, resolve me:
Have you a mistress, or a wife?
Eroclea. I have neither. 275
Kala. Nor did you ever love in earnest any
Fair lady whom you wished to make your own?
Eroclea. Not any, truly.
Kala. What your friends or means are
I will not be inquisitive to know,
Nor do I care to hope for. But admit 280
A dower were thrown down before your choice,
Of beauty, noble birth, and sincere affection,
How gladly would you entertain it? Young man,
I do not tempt you idly.
Eroclea. I shall thank you
When my unsettled thoughts can make me sensible 285
Of what 'tis to be happy; for the present
I am your debtor; and, fair gentlewoman,
Pray give me leave as yet to study ignorance
For my weak brains conceive not what concerns me.
——Another time——

Enter THAMASTA.

Thamasta. Do I break off your parley 290
That you are parting? Sure, my woman loves you.
Can she speak well, Parthenophill?
Eroclea. Yes, madam,

271. *Aside*] Gifford. *(Kala) Aside*] This ed. 272.1. *stay*] stayes Q. 282. and sincere] Q; sincere Weber. 289. concerns] Weber; concerne Q.

---

273 *May ... sir?*] I hope I am not troubling you, sir.
274. *resolve me*] make clear to me.
288. *study ignorance*] try to be as if ignorant (of your offer); 'study': aim at, be solicitous of (*O.E.D.*, vb.II.11).

D

> Discreetly chaste she can; she hath much won
> On my belief, and in few words, but pithy,
> Much moved my thankfulness. You are her lady; 295
> Your goodness aims, I know, at her preferment;
> Therefore I may be bold to make confession
> Of truth: if ever I desire to thrive
> In woman's favour Kala is the first
> Whom my ambition shall bend to.
>
> *Thamasta.*   Indeed! 300
> But say a nobler love should interpose?
>
> *Eroclea.* Where real worth and constancy first settle
> A hearty truth, there greatness cannot shake it,
> Nor shall it mine. Yet I am but an infant
> In that construction which must give clear light 305
> To Kala's merit; riper hours hereafter
> Must learn me how to grow rich in deserts.
> Madam, my duty waits on you   *Exit* EROCLEA.
>
> *Thamasta.*   Come hither.
> 'If ever henceforth I desire to thrive
> In woman's favours, Kala is the first 310
> Whom my ambition shall bend to.'——'Twas so?
>
> *Kala.* These very words he spake.
>
> *Thamasta.*   These very words
> Curse thee, unfaithful creature, to thy grave.
> Thou wood'st him for thyself?
>
> *Kala.*   You said I should.
>
> *Thamasta.* My name was never mentioned?
>   Madam, no; 315

293-4. *much . . . belief*] greatly increased my trust.

302-7.] Eroclea extricates herself from an awkward situation by gently snubbing Thamasta and Kala under the guise of courtly evasions. In ll. 302-4 she asserts that greatness (i.e. 'a nobler love') cannot break any pledge of hers provided that its recipient proves a worthy and constant lover. However, she cannot yet interpret ('construction': interpretation) Kala well enough to know if she deserves that description (ll. 304-6). Having thus defended the integrity of the conditional pledge she made to Kala in ll. 297-300, and at the same time left a way open for withdrawal, in ll. 306-7 she guardedly addresses herself to the nobler love proposed by Thamasta. Subsequent, more mature, consideration must teach her (1) how to become deserving enough (for Thamasta), or, more evasively, (2) how to make the best of what is due to her own merits. 'Learn' (l. 307), used transitively for 'teach', was a frequent and not vulgar usage.

314. *wood'st*] didst woo.

SC II]   THE LOVER'S MELANCHOLY   85

Kala.
    We were not come to that.
Thamasta.   Not come to that!
    Art thou a rival fit to cross my fate?
    Now poverty and dishonest fame,
    The waiting-woman's wages, be thy payment.
    False, faithless, wanton beast, I'll spoil your carriage;   320
    There's not a page, a groom, nay, not a citizen
    That shall be cast upon ye, Kala,
    I'll keep thee in my service all thy lifetime
    Without hope of a husband or a suitor.
Kala. I have not verily deserved this cruelty.   325
Thamasta. Parthenophill shall know, if he respect
    My birth, the danger of a fond neglect. *Exit* THAMASTA.
Kala. Are you so quick? Well, I may chance to cross
    Your peevishness. Now, though I never meant
    The young man for myself, yet if he love me   330
    I'll have him, or I'll run away with him,
    And let her do her worst then. What! we are all
    But flesh and blood; the same thing that will do
    My lady good will please her woman too.   *Exit.*

ACT II SCENE ii

Enter CLEOPHILA *and* TROLLIO.

Cleophila. Tread softly, Trollio, my father sleeps still.
Trollio. Ay, forsooth; but he sleeps like a hare with his eyes
    open and that's no good sign.
Cleophila. Sure, thou art weary of this sullen living

320. carriage] Q; marriage *Ellis, conj. Gifford, Dyce.*

---

   320. *carriage*] proceedings (*O.E.D.*, II.16). Ellis emends to 'marriage', which is persuasive, but Q's reading makes satisfactory sense.
   326. *respect*] consider.
   327. *fond*] foolish.
   328. *quick*] hasty.
   333–4. *the . . . too*] This looks, but apparently is not, proverbial. Tilley's maid/mistress group of proverbs does not include Kala's version of 'What is sauce for the goose is sauce for the gander.'

   2–3. *sleeps . . . open*] proverbial (Tilley, H 153); the hare was supposed to be the most timid of animals and therefore always watchful.
   4. *sullen*] melancholy.

86   THE LOVER'S MELANCHOLY   [ACT II

      But I am not; for I take more content   5
      In my obedience here than all delights
      The time presents elsewhere.
Meleander. Within.   O!
Cleophila.   Dost hear that groan?
Trollio. Hear it! I shudder. It was a strong blast, young
      mistress, able to root up heart, liver, lungs, and all.
Cleophila. My much-wronged father! Let me view his face.   10

      Draws the arras; MELEANDER *discovered in a chair sleeping.*

Trollio. Lady mistress, shall I fetch a barber to steal away his
      rough beard whiles he sleeps in's naps? He never looks in a
      glass and 'tis high time, on conscience, for him to be
      trimmed; 'has not been under the shaver's hand almost
      these four years.   15
Cleophila. Peace, fool!
Trollio. [*Aside.*] I could clip the old ruffian; there's hair
      enough to stuff all the great codpieces in Switzerland. 'A
      begins to stir, 'a stirs. Bless us, how his eyes roll! [*To him.*]
      A goodyear keep your lordship in your right wits, I   20

7. *Meleander*] *Menander Q.*   12. sleeps in's naps? He] *Q;* sleeps? In his naps
he *Gifford.*   17. *Aside*] *Gifford.*   19. *To him*] *This ed.*

10.1.] Meleander was probably concealed within a 'discovery space', a shallow area within an open tiring house doorway in front of which curtains had been hung. See Richard Hosley's discussion of the first Globe and second Blackfriars playhouses in *Revels History*, pp. 175–235, especially pp. 184–8, 195, 220–2, 226. Little is known about the second Globe playhouse but presumably the same arrangement for discoveries obtained there.

13. *on conscience*] in reason or fairness; the phrase is usually 'in' or 'of' conscience.

14–15. *'has ... years*] Trollio must be exaggerating since Eroclea was absent for only two years (cf. II.i.197–198) and Meleander's distresses could hardly have begun long before her flight from the wicked designs of Palador's father. The uncut hair after the loss of a daughter recalls the grief of Pericles (*Pericles*, IV.iv.27–8).

18. *codpieces*] a padded and often ornamented appendage at the fork of men's hose or breeches; it went out of fashion after 1600, hence the use of the word in a jocular context both here and at V.i.132–3 (Linthicum, pp. 204–5).

20. *goodyear*] common term of uncertain significance; *O.E.D.* (a, b) suggests that the expletive form, 'What the good year', was equated with, 'What the devil', so that goodyear came to denote some malefic power; this sense is supported by the identification with 'goodger(s)', i.e. the devil, in *The English Dialect Dictionary*. Hanmer's derivation of the term in 'The good years shall devour them, flesh and fell' (*Lear*, V.iii.24) from the French

SC II]   THE LOVER'S MELANCHOLY   87

    beseech ye!
Meleander. Cleophila!
Cleophila.   Sir, I am here; how d'ee, sir?
Trollio. Sir, is your stomach up yet? Get some warm porridge
    in your belly, 'tis a very good settle-brain.
Meleander. The raven croaked and hollow shrieks of owls   25
    Sung dirges at her funeral; I laughed
    The whiles for 'twas no boot to weep. The girl
    Was fresh and full of youth; but, O! the cunning
    Of tyrants that look big—their very frowns
    Doom poor souls guilty ere their cause be heard.   30
    Good, what art thou? and thou?
Cleophila.   I am Cleophila,
    Your woeful daughter.
Trollio.   I am Trollio,
    Your honest implement.
Meleander. I know ye both. 'Las, why d'ee use me thus?
    Thy sister, my Eroclea, was so gentle   35
    That turtles in their down do feed more gall
    Than her spleen mixed with; yet, when winds and storm
    Drive dirt and dust on banks of spotless snow,
    The purest whiteness is no such defence
    Against the sullying foulness of that fury.   40
    So raved Agenor, that great man, mischief
    Against the girl——'twas a politic trick,
    We were too old in honour——I am lean
    And fallen away extremely; most assuredly
    I have not dined these three days.
Cleophila.   Will you now, sir?   45

'goujeres, the pox' (which he hypothetically derived from 'gouje', a camp-follower) is very doubtful.
    23. *stomach*] appetite.
    27. *no boot*] useless.
    32. *Trollio*] Q reads 'Trollia' which may possibly be a deliberate spelling intended to underline his comic echoing of Cleophila's doleful remark.
    33. *implement*] instrument. Applied to a person this is the earliest citation in O.E.D. (sb.1.2.b).
    36–7. *turtles . . . with*] Young doves nourish more ill-feeling than her spleen has had to do with. 'Down' refers to the first feathering of young birds; the spleen was regarded as the seat of melancholy, violent, spiteful feelings.
    43. *We . . . honour*] This presumably means that Meleander and his family were too accustomed to honourable dealings to suspect that Agenor's betrothal of Palador to Eroclea was a cover for his own designs on her.

Trollio. I beseech ye heartily, sir. I feel a horrible puking myself.
Meleander. Am I stark mad?
Trollio. No, no, you are but a little staring——there's difference between staring and stark mad. You are but whimsied yet, crotchetted, conundrumed, or so.
Meleander. Here's all my care; and I do often sigh
For thee, Cleophila; we are secluded
From all good people. But take heed; Amethus
Was son to Doryla, Agenor's sister.
There's some ill blood about him, if the surgeon
Have not been very skilful to let all out.
Cleophila. I am, alas, too grieved to think of love;
That must concern me least.
Meleander. Sirrah, be wise, be wise.
Trollio. Who I? I will be monstrous and wise immediately.

Enter AMETHUS, MENAPHON, EROCLEA *as before, and* RHETIAS.

Welcome, gentlemen, the more the merrier. I'll lay the cloth and set the stools in a readiness, for I see here is some hope of dinner now.

Exit TROLLIO.

Amethus. My Lord Meleander, Menaphon, your kinsman,
Newly returned from travel, comes to tender
His duty t'ee; to you his love, fair mistress.
Menaphon. I would I could as easily remove
Sadness from your remembrance, sir, as study
To do you faithful service——My dear cousin,
All best of comforts bless your sweet obedience!
Cleophila. One chief of 'em, worthy cousin, lives
In you and your well-doing.
Menaphon. This young stranger
Will well deserve your knowledge.
Amethus. For my friend's sake,
Lady, pray give him welcome.
Cleophila. He has met it,

60.1.] Dyce subst.; after l. 59 Q. 71. worthy] Q; my worthy Weber.

---

51. *whimsied . . . crotchetted, conundrumed*] roughly synonymous terms; 'filled with freakish, perverse and crazy notions'. Q reads 'conundroun'd' so possibly a clown's confusion, 'conundrowned', was intended.

If sorrows can look kindly.
Eroclea. You much honour me. 75
Rhetias. [*Aside*] How 'a eyes the company! Sure my passion
    will betray my weakness——[*To Meleander.*] O my
    master, my noble master, do not forget me; I am still the
    humblest and the most faithful in heart of those that serve
    you. 80
Meleander. Ha! ha! ha!
Rhetias. [*Aside.*] There's wormwood in that laughter; 'tis the
    usher to a violent extremity.
Meleander. I am a weak old man. All these are come
    To jeer my ripe calamities.
Menaphon. Good uncle! 85
Meleander. But I'll outstare 'ee all; fools, desperate fools!
    You are cheated, grossly cheated; range, range on,
    And roll about the world to gather moss,
    The moss of honour, gay reports, gay clothes,
    Gay wives, huge empty buildings, whose proud roofs 90
    Shall with their pinnacles even reach the stars.
    Ye work and work like moles, blind in the paths
    That are bored through the crannies of the earth,
    To charge your hungry souls with such full surfeits
    As being gorged once, make 'ee lean with plenty. 95
    And when ye have skimmed the vomit of your riots,
    Y'are fat in no felicity but folly;
    Then your last sleeps seize on 'ee. Then the troops
    Of worms crawl round and feast; good cheer, rich fare,

76. *Aside*] Gifford.   77. *To Meleander*] *This ed.*   82. *Aside*] Gifford.   92. moles, blind] *Q;* blind moles, *Gifford.*

---

76. *'a*] he; i.e. Meleander.
76–7. *my . . . weakness*] The storm of my feelings will force me to reveal my tenderness of heart (contrary to his assumed bluntness).
82. *wormwood*] medicinal herb of bitter flavour.
88.] This is an odd statement given the proverb it recalls, 'A rolling stone gathers no moss' (Tilley, S 885). Perhaps Meleander is satirically reversing the proverb to make a point about the worthlessness of the 'moss' that man spends his life in gathering.
95. *make . . . plenty*] i.e. because worldly pleasures are unsatisfying.
96. *skimmed . . . riots*] The rapaciousness of appetite for worldly satisfactions is nauseatingly imaged here; surfeit produces vomiting and the richest part of this is greedily devoured.

Dainty, delicious——Here's Cleophila, 100
All the poor stock of my remaining thrift.
You, you, the prince's cousin, how d'ee like her?
Amethus, how d'ee like her?
Amethus.   My intents
Are just and honourable.
Menaphon.   Sir, believe him.
Meleander. Take her——We two must part; go to him, do. 105
Eroclea. This sight is full of horror.
Rhetias.   There is sense yet
In this distraction.
Meleander. In this jewel I have given away
All what I can call mine. When I am dead
Save charge; let me be buried in a nook. 110
No guns, no pompous whining; these are fooleries.
If, whiles we live, we stalk about the streets
Justled by carmen, footposts, and fine apes
In silken coats, unminded and scarce thought on,
It is not comely to be haled to the earth 115
Like high-fed jades upon a tilting day,
In antic trappings. Scorn to useless tears!
Eroclea was not coffined so; she perished
And no eye dropped save mine, and I am childish.
I talk like one that dotes. Laugh at me, Rhetias, 120
Or rail at me. They will not give me meat,
They have starved me; but I'll henceforth be mine own
    cook.
Good morrow! 'Tis too early for my cares

---

106. There] *Weber;* This *Q.*

106–7. There ... distraction] probably an echo of *Lear,* IV.vi.175–6, 'O, matter and impertinency mix'd! Reason in madness!' See Introduction, p. 8.
    113. *carmen*] carters.
    footposts] messengers on foot.
    116–17. *Like ... trappings*] Horses and riders were richly adorned for tilts. On the pageantry of tilt days see Sir E. K. Chambers, *The Elizabethan Stage* (4 vols., Oxford, 1923), I, 139–48.
    jades] horses; jade is usually contemptuous, to denote an ill-tempered or worn-out horse, or one of inferior breed.
    117. *Scorn ... tears*] The expanded sense of this forceful ellipsis might be, 'Such pomp-laden burials make a mockery of tears which are in any case unavailing'; or, as E. A. J. Honigmann suggests, '(I have nothing but) scorn for useless tears.'

SC II]   THE LOVER'S MELANCHOLY   91

  To revel. I will break my heart a little,
  And tell ye more hereafter. Pray be merry. 125
       Exit MELEANDER.
Rhetias. I'll follow him. [*Aside.*] My Lord Amethus, use your
  time
  Respectively. Few words to purpose soon'st prevail;
  Study no long orations; be plain and short.
  [*To them.*] I'll follow him. *Exit* RHETIAS.
Amethus. Cleophila, although these blacker clouds 130
  Of sadness thicken and make dark the sky
  Of thy fair eyes, yet give me leave to follow
  The stream of my affections; they are pure,
  Without all mixture of unnoble thoughts.
  Can you be ever mine?
Cleophila.   I am so low 135
  In mine own fortunes and my father's woes
  That I want words to tell ye you deserve
  A worthier choice.
Amethus.   But give me leave to hope.
Menaphon. My friend is serious.
Cleophila.   Sir, this for answer:
  If I ever thrive in an earthly happiness, 140
  The next to my good father's wished recovery
  Must be my thankfulness to your great merit,
  Which I dare promise; for the present time
  You cannot urge more from me.
Meleander. [*Within.*] Ho, Cleophila!
Cleophila. This gentleman is moved.
Amethus.   Your eyes, Parthenophill, 145
  Are guilty of some passion.
Menaphon.   Friend, what ails thee?
Eroclea. All is not well within me, sir.
Meleander Within.   Cleophila!

126. *Aside*] This ed. 129. *To them*] This ed. 139–41.] This ed.; *Q*. prints . . . serious. / . . . thriue / . . . next / . . . recouery, 143. promise; for . . . time] *So Dyce;* promise for . . . time: *Q.* 144. *Within*] Weber.

---

 124. *revel*] be freely expressed.
 127. *Respectively*] carefully.
 146. *guilty . . . passion*] show signs of suffering. Cf. I.iii.65 for Eroclea's betrayal of her feelings.

Amethus. Sweet maid, forget me not; we now must part.
Cleophila. Still you shall have my prayer.
Amethus. Still you my truth.
Exeunt omnes.

149.1. *Exeunt omnes*] Exeunt omnes. | *Finis Actus secundi.* Q.

Act III

ACT III SCENE i

Enter CUCULUS *and* GRILLA, CUCULUS *in a black velvet cap and a white feather, with a paper in his hand.*

Cuculus. Do not I look freshly, and like a youth of the trim?
Grilla. As rare an old youth as ever walked cross-gartered.
Cuculus. Here are my mistresses mustered in white and black. [*Reads.*] 'Kala, the waiting-woman'. I will first begin at the foot. Stand thou for Kala. 5
Grilla. I stand for Kala; do your best and your worst.
Cuculus. I must look big, and care little or nothing for her, because she is a creature that stands at livery. Thus I talk wisely, and to no purpose: wench, as it is not fit that thou shouldst be either fair or honest, so, considering thy 10 service, thou art as thou art; and so are thy betters, let them be what they can be. Thus, in despite and defiance of all thy good parts, if I cannot endure thy baseness 'tis more out of thy courtesy than my deserving; and so I expect thy answer. 15
Grilla. I must confess——

Act III] Actus III. Scena I. Q.   4. *Reads*] Weber.

---

1. *youth . . . trim*] See note to I.iii.2.
2. *cross-gartered*] The garter was placed below the knee in front, crossed behind the knee, brought forward above the knee and tied with a bow; cross-gartering became increasingly unfashionable after 1600, hence Grilla's gibe (Linthicum, p. 264).
7. *big*] haughty.
8. *stands at livery*] The primary reference is to Kala's servant status but the phrasing also connects her with the stabling of horses, implying that she is his kept woman (*O.E.D.*, sb.10.a(c)). Cf. Massinger's *City Madam*, I.iii.8, 'a Liverie punk, or so'.
13–14. *'tis . . . deserving*] nonsense use of common formula (Tilley, C 337). Cf. *The Queen*, ll. 3041–2 (ed. W. Bang, *Materialien zur Kunde des älteren Englischen Dramas* (Louvain), vol. XIII, 1906).

Cuculus. Well said.
Grilla. You are——
Cuculus. That's true too.
Grilla. To speak you right, a very scurvy fellow—— 20
Cuculus. Away, away! Dost think so?
Grilla. A very foul-mouthed and misshapen coxcomb.
Cuculus. I'll never believe it, by this hand.
Grilla. A maggot, most unworthy to creep in——to the least
  wrinkle of a gentlewoman's, what d'ee call, good conceit, 25
  or so, or what you will else——were you not refined by
  courtship and education, which, in my blear eyes, makes
  you appear as sweet as any nosegay, or savoury cod of
  musk new fallen from th'cat.
Cuculus. This shall serve well enough for the waiting-woman. 30
  My next mistress is Cleophila, the old madman's daughter. I must come to her in whining tune, sigh, wipe mine
  eyes, fold my arms, and blubber out my speech as thus:
  even as a kennel of hounds, sweet lady, cannot catch a hare
  when they are full paunched on the carrion of a dead 35
  horse; so, even so, the gorge of my affections being full
  crammed with the garboils of your condolements, doth
  tickle me with the prick, as it were, about me, and fellow-
  feeling of howling outright.
Grilla. This will do't, if we will hear. 40
Cuculus. Thou see'st I am crying ripe; I am such another
  tender-hearted fool.
Grilla. Even as the snuff of a candle that is burnt in the socket

---

24–9.] *This ed.; verse in* Q ... in—— / ... Gentlewomans / ... what / ... Courtship / ... eyes / ... nosegay, / ... Cat.

---

25. *conceit*] opinion. A bawdy pun seems also intended, i.e. that which conceives, although this sense is not given in Partridge or *O.E.D.*

28–9. *cod of musk*] musk-bag; the sac containing the glands of the musk cat or civet from which perfume is extracted.

34–9. *even ... outright*] This absurd comparison mocks both Cuculus and the euphuistic style from which it derives. Cf. ll. 43–9 below.

37. *garboils ... condolements*] tumult of your lamentations.

38–9. *tickle ... outright*] He is goaded on to weep out of sympathy with Cleophila.

40.] This will prevail upon me if I grant you attention. Gifford suggests that 'we' is probably a misprint for 'she', but since Grilla is answering throughout this exchange in the first peron, I retain 'we' as a royal plural, although it is true that Grilla does not use it when speaking for Thamasta.

goes out and leaves a strong perfume behind it; or as a
piece of toasted cheese next the heart in a morning is a
restorative for a sweet breath; so, even so, the odoriferous
savour of your love doth perfume my heart—heigh-ho!—
with the pure scent of an intolerable content, and not to be
endured.
Cuculus. By this hand, 'tis excellent. Have at thee, last of all,
for the Princess Thamasta, she that is my mistress indeed.
She is abominably proud, a lady of a damnable, high,
turbulent, and generous spirit; but I have a loud-mouthed
cannon of mine own to batter her, and a penned speech of
purpose. Observe it.
Grilla. Thus I walk by, hear, and mind you not.
Cuculus. [*Reads.*] 'Though haughty as the devil or his dam
Thou dost appear, great mistress, yet I am
Like to an ugly firework, and can mount
Above the region of thy sweet ac——count.
Wert thou the moon herself, yet having seen thee,
Behold the man ordained to move within thee.'
——Look to yourself, housewife! Answer me in strong
lines, y'are best.
Grilla. Keep off, poor fool, my beams will strike thee blind;
Else, if thou touch me, touch me but behind.
In palaces, such as pass in before
Must be great princes; for at the back door
Tatterdemalions wait, who know not how
To get admittance; such a one——art thou.
Cuculus. 'Sfoot, this is downright roaring.

57. *Reads*] *So Gifford.*

---

56. *mind you not*] ignore you.
   60. *ac——count*] Cuculus breaks the word to throw stress upon 'count' and bring out the sexual pun; the bawdy innuendo is continued in l. 62 and in Grilla's reply.
   63. *strong lines*] contemporary term, which Cuculus ignorantly parrots, for the conceits and obscurities of the metaphysical style.
   64. *y'are best*] indicative for subjunctive 'you were'. Other editors emend, but Ford uses 'y'are best' at III.ii.12; cf. *'Tis Pity* (ed. Roper), II.i.15.
   68. *back door*] For the obscene sense cf. *The Insatiate Countess*, II.ii.70–3 (*Works of John Marston*, ed. A. H. Bullen (London, 1887), vol. III).
   71. *'Sfoot*] God's foot.
   roaring] reference to 'roaring boys', riotous gallants. Middleton and Rowley's *A Fair Quarrel* (1617) has a comic 'roaring school'.

96   THE LOVER'S MELANCHOLY   [ACT III

Grilla. I know how to present a big lady in her own cue. But,
pray, in earnest, are you in love with all these?
Cuculus. Pish, I have not a rag of love about me. 'Tis only a
foolish humour I am possessed with, to be surnamed the   75
Conquerer. I will court anything; be in love with nothing,
nor no——thing.
Grilla. A rare man you are, I protest.
Cuculus. Yes, I know I am a rare man, and I ever held myself
so.   80

Enter PELIAS *and* CORAX.

Pelias. In amorous contemplation, on my life;
Courting his page, by Helicon!
Cuculus.   'Tis false.
Grilla. A gross untruth; I'll justify it, sir,
At any time, place, weapon.
Cuculus.   Marry, shall she.
Corax. No quarrels, goody Whisk. Lay by your trumperies   85
and fall to your practice. Instructions are ready for you all.
Pelias is your leader; follow him. Get credit now or never.
Vanish, doodles, vanish.
Cuculus. For the device?
Corax. The same; get 'ee gone, and make no bawling.   90
          Exeunt [all but CORAX*].*
To waste my time thus drone-like in the court,
And lose so many hours as my studies
Have hoarded up, is to be like a man

85. goody] *Gifford;* good'ee *Q.*   90.1. all but CORAX] *Weber.*

---

72. *own cue*] proper disposition. The connection with French 'queue'
(O.Fr. 'cue') suggests, in this context, the common bawdy pun on 'tail'
(Partridge, p. 196).
   75–6. *surnamed the Conqueror*] comic allusion to William I of England;
perhaps also to 'Caesar's thrasonical brag of "I came, saw, and overcame"'
(*A.Y.L.*, V.ii.29–31). Cuculus' conquests are to be sexual, and given the
bawdy puns sprinkling this episode 'Con-que-ror' also looks suspect.
   77. *no——thing*] 'thing': pudendum (Partridge, p. 199). The play on
'nothing' may also include the sense of 'naught' i.e. sexual immorality.
   82. *Helicon*] mountain in Greece, sacred to the muses.
   85. *goody*] goodwife.
Whisk] whipper-snapper.
trumperies] trifling.
   88. *doodles*] simpletons, noodles.
   89. *device*] masque.

That creeps both on his hands and knees to climb
A mountain's top; where, when he is ascended, 95
One careless slip down tumbles him again
Into the bottom whence 'a first began.
I need no prince's favour; princes need
My art. Then, Corax, be no more a gull;
The best of 'em cannot fool thee, nay, they shall not. 100

Enter SOPHRONOS *and* ARETUS.

Sophronos. We find him timely now; let's learn the cause.
Aretus. 'Tis fit we should——Sir, we approve you learnèd
And since your skill can best discern the humours
That are predominant in bodies subject
To alteration, tell us, pray, what devil 105
This melancholy is which can transform
Men into monsters.
Corax.   Y'are yourself a scholar,
And quick of apprehension. Melancholy
Is not as you conceive, indisposition
Of body, but the mind's disease. So ecstasy, 110
Fantastic dotage, madness, phrenzy, rapture
Of mere imagination, differ partly
From melancholy, which is briefly this:
A mere commotion of the mind, o'ercharged

109. conceive, indisposition] *Weber;* conceiue. Indisposition *Q.* 111. rapture] *Dyce;* Rupture *Q.* 113–14.] *Q. has marginal note:* Vid. De- / mocrit. Iu- / nior.

103–7. And ... monsters] According to renaissance physiology and psychology any imbalance of the four primary humours (blood, choler, melancholy, phlegm) which constituted a man's temperament would produce pathological conditions.

108–18. Melancholy ... affection] In correcting Aretus Corax is only half-right since although melancholy is certainly a disease of the mind it was thought to have its roots in a physical condition, abnormality of the melancholy humour; this abnormality itself may be provoked by physical or psychological causes. Babb writes, 'The melancholic malady is fundamentally a physical condition. Yet its symptoms are so largely psychological that it is ordinarily regarded as a mental disease' (p. 23). This passage is closely indebted to Burton, as Ford's marginal note, '*Vid. Democrit. Iunior.*', to these lines indicates. See Burton, pp. 119–20, 148–51; I: I: I: 2, 3; and I: I: 3: I, 2.

111. *dotage*] mental derangement; not here associated with old age, nor by Burton (p. 121; I: I: I: 4). Cf. III.iii.45.

112. *mere*] sole, alone.

	With fear and sorrow, first begot i'th' brain,	115
	The seat of reason, and from thence derived	
	As suddenly into the heart, the seat	
	Of our affection.	

Aretus.   There are sundry kinds
    Of this disturbance?
Corax.   Infinite; it were
    More easy to conjecture every hour   120
    We have to live, than reckon up the kinds
    Or causes of this anguish of the mind.
Sophronos. Thus you conclude that as the cause is doubtful
    The cure must be impossible; and then
    Our prince, poor gentleman, is lost for ever,   125
    As well unto himself as to his subjects.
Corax. My lord, you are too quick. Thus much I dare
    Promise and do; ere many minutes pass
    I will discover whence his sadness is,
    Or undergo the censure of my ignorance.   130
Aretus. You are a noble scholar.
Sophronos.   For reward,
    You shall make your own demand.
Corax.   May I be sure?
Aretus. We both will pledge our truth.
Corax.   'Tis soon performed:
    That I may be discharged from my attendance
    At court, and never more be sent for after;   135
    Or, if I be, may rats gnaw all my books,
    If I get home once and come here again.
    Though my neck stretch a halter for't, I care not.
Sophronos. Come, come, you shall not fear it.
Corax.   I'll acquaint ye
    With what is to be done, and you shall fashion it.   140
                                     Exeunt omnes.

---

    116. *derived*] transmitted.
    129. *discover*] 'reveal' (*O.E.D.*, 3.4) rather than 'find out'; cf. IV.i.30. The way that Corax leads Palador through the masque of melancholy to confront him finally with love melancholy (III.iii.94–111) suggests that Corax, like Hamlet with his 'mouse-trap', merely requires confirmation of what is almost a certainty in his mind.

ACT III   SCENE ii

Enter KALA *and* EROCLEA *as before.*

Kala. My lady does expect 'ee, thinks all time
   Too slow till you come to her. Wherefore, young man,
   If you intend to love me, and me only,
   Before we part, without more circumstance,
   Let us betroth ourselves.
Eroclea.   I dare not wrong 'ee;   5
   You are too violent.
Kala.   Wrong me no more
   Than I wrong you; be mine, and I am yours.
   I cannot stand on points.
Eroclea.   Then, to resolve
   All further hopes, you never can be mine,
   Must not, and—pardon though I say—you shall not.   10
Kala. [*Aside.*] The thing is sure a gelding——[*To her.*] Shall
   not? Well,
   Y'are best to prate unto my lady now
   What proffer I have made.
Eroclea.   Never, I vow.
Kala. Do, do; 'tis but a kind heart of mine own,
   And ill luck can undo me——[*Aside.*] Be refused!   15
   O scurvy!——[*To her.*] Pray walk on, I'll overtake 'ee.
                                             Exit EROCLEA.
   What a green-sickness-livered boy is this!
   My maidenhead will shortly grow so stale
   That 'twill be mouldy; but I'll mar her market.

                  Enter MENAPHON.

11. *Aside*] Weber.   *To her*] *This ed.*   15. *Aside*] *This ed.*   16. *To her*] *This ed.*   16.1. *Exit* EROCLEA] *Weber; after l. 17 Q.*

---

8. *stand on points*] be concerned about niceties.
11. *gelding*] eunuch.
12. *Y'are best*] Cf. III.i.64 and note.
14–15. *'tis . . . me*] Kala means, I take it, that her only fault in the matter is her susceptibility of feelings which can easily be misplaced and thus ruin her.
17. *green-sickness-livered*] Properly an anaemic affliction of young women but here the term impugns Parthenophill's virility. The liver was supposed to be the seat of sexual passion.
19. *her market*] Thamasta's chances with Parthenophill, and perhaps also with Menaphon.

Menaphon. Parthenophill passed this way; prithee, Kala, 20
    Direct me to him.
Kala.   Yes, I can direct 'ee;
    But you, sir, must forbear.
Menaphon.   Forbear!
Kala.   I said so.
    Your bounty has engaged my truth; receive
    A secret that will, as you are a man,
    Startle your reason; 'tis but mere respect   2
    Of what I owe to thankfulness. Dear sir,
    The stranger whom your courtesy received
    For friend is made your rival.
Menaphon.   Rival, Kala!
    Take heed, thou art too credulous.
Kala.   My lady
    Dotes on him. I will place you in a room   30
    Where, though you cannot hear, yet you shall see
    Such passages as will confirm the truth
    Of my intelligence.
Menaphon.   'Twill make me mad.
Kala. Yes, yes. It makes me mad, too, that a gentleman
    So excellently sweet, so liberal,   35
    So kind, so proper, should be so betrayed
    By a young smooth-chinned straggler. But, for love's sake,
    Bear all with manly courage——Not a word;
    I am undone then.
Menaphon.   That were too much pity.
    Honest, most honest Kala, 'tis thy care,   40
    Thy serviceable care.
Kala.   You have even spoken
    All can be said or thought.
Menaphon.   I will reward thee.

20. this] *Weber;* the *Q.*

    25–6. *respect . . . thankfulness*] regard for what gratitude demands.
    37. *straggler*] interloper; the more common sense is 'vagabond'; cf. III.ii.191.
    39. *I . . . then*] or I shall be ruined.
    40–2. *Honest . . . thought*] Menaphon believes that Kala's only interest in the matter is one of sincere service, and she lyingly confirms that this is indeed the whole truth about her motivation.

                    But as for him, ungentle boy, I'll whip
                    His falsehood with a vengeance——
Kala.   O, speak little.
                    Walk up these stairs; and take this key; it opens   45
                    A chamber door where, at that window yonder,
                    You may see all their courtship.
Menaphon.   I am silent.
Kala. As little noise as may be, I beseech ye;
                    There is a back-stair to convey ye forth
                    Unseen or unsuspected.   *Exit* MENAPHON.
                                     He that cheats   50
                    A waiting-woman of a free good turn
                    She longs for must expect a shrewd revenge.
                    Sheep-spirited boy! Although he had not married me,
                    He might have proffered kindness in a corner
                    And ne'er have been the worse for't. They are come;   55
                    On goes my set of faces most demurely.

                         Enter THAMASTA, *and* EROCLEA [*as before*].

Thamasta. Forbear the room.
Kala.   Yes, madam.
Thamasta.   Whosoever
                    Requires access to me deny him entrance
                    Till I call thee; and wait without.
Kala.   I shall.

50. unsuspected.] vnsuspected.——Q.   *Exit* MENAPHON] *Weber; after l.* 47 Q.   56.1 *as before*] *This ed.*   57–61.] *Weber; prose in* Q.

45–50.] Kala is presumably directing Menaphon through one of the stage doors to stairs within the tiring house, leading to a windowed gallery in the tiring house wall overlooking the stage. See Richard Hosley's discussion of 'actions above' in *Revels History*, especially pp. 188–90, 195, 222–4, 226. The 'back-stair' is probably just a fictional part of the clandestine arrangements; when Menaphon re-enters later in the scene it could be at another door conventionally designated as from without, rather than from within, the house.

51. *good turn*] sexual; see Partridge, p. 207.

52. *shrewd*] grievous.

56.] The general sense that Kala is going to put on a show to cover her deception is clear, but 'set of faces' is an odd phrase; 'set face' would seem more appropriate. However, *Lady's Trial*, II.i; vol. III, 27, has 'set of looks' referring to a courtier's choice of countenance. Kala must mean that she has a collection of faces, all hypocritical, ready to select from in continuing her deception of Thamasta.

[*Aside*.] Sweet Venus, turn his courage to a snowball, 60
I heartily beseech it. *Exit.*
Thamasta. I expose
The honour of my birth, my fame, my youth,
To hazard of much hard construction
In seeking an adventure of a parley
So private with a stranger. If your thoughts 65
Censure me not with mercy, you may soon
Conceive I have laid by that modesty
Which should preserve a virtuous name unstained.
Eroclea. Lady—to shorten long excuses—time
And safe experience have so throughly armed 70
My apprehension with a real taste
Of your most noble nature, that to question
The least part of your bounties, or that freedom
Which heaven hath with a plenty made you rich in,
Would argue me uncivil; which is more, 75
Base-bred; and which is most of all, unthankful.
Thamasta. The constant lodestone and the steel are found
In several mines, yet is there such a league
Between these minerals, as if one vein
Of earth had nourished both. The gentle myrtle 80
Is not engraft upon an olive's stock,
Yet nature hath between them locked a secret
Of sympathy, that, being planted near,
They will both in their branches and their roots
Embrace each other. Twines of ivy round 85
The well-grown oak; the vine doth court the elm;
Yet these are different plants. Parthenophill,
Consider this aright, then these slight creatures
Will fortify the reasons I should frame

60. *Aside*] Weber.

63.] to the risk of unfavourable interpretation.
71. *apprehension*] understanding.
real] dissyllabic.

77–87.] This passage is close to Burton (p. 622; 3: 1: 1: 2) where he writes of the natural love or hatred to be observed in both animate and inanimate creatures; of Ford's examples only the ivy and oak are not mentioned by Burton.

78. *several*] separate.
85. *round*] encircle.
86. *vine . . . elm*] proverbial (Tilley, V 61).

> For that ungrounded—as thou think'st—affection 90
> Which is submitted to a stranger's pity.
> True love may blush when shame repents too late,
> But in all actions, nature yields to fate.
>
> *Eroclea.* Great lady, 'twere a dulness must exceed
> The grossest and most sottish kind of ignorance 95
> Not to be sensible of your intents;
> I clearly understand them. Yet so much
> The difference between that height and lowness
> Which doth distinguish our unequal fortunes
> Dissuades me from ambition, that I am 100
> Humbler in my desires than love's own power
> Can any way raise up.
>
> *Thamasta.*   I am a princess,
> And know no law of slavery; to sue,
> Yet be denied?
>
> *Eroclea.*   I am so much a subject
> To every law of noble honesty, 105
> That to transgress the vows of perfect friendship
> I hold a sacrilege as foul and cursed
> As if some holy temple had been robbed
> And I the thief.
>
> *Thamasta.*   Thou art unwise, young man,
> To enrage a lioness.
>
> *Eroclea.*   It were unjust 110
> To falsify a faith, and ever after,
> Disrobed of that fair ornament, live naked,
> A scorn to time and truth.
>
> *Thamasta.*   Remember well
> Who I am and what thou art.
>
> *Eroclea.*   That remembrance
> Prompts me to worthy duty. O great lady, 115
> If some few days have tempted your free heart

92–3.] Thamasta, having defended her suit to Parthenophill by analogies in nature, then admits that she may have over-stepped the bounds of modesty, her excuse now being the necessity of fate.

103. *know . . . slavery*] 'know' means 'acknowledge' (*O.E.D.*, vb. I.2). The condition of being a slave—begging and being denied—is rejected by Thamasta. Eroclea's reply, that she by contrast does acknowledge the force of vows and laws, is a clever rebuke.

106. *perfect friendship*] i.e. with Menaphon.

116. *free*] noble.

   To cast away affection on a stranger;
   If that affection have so oversway'd
   Your judgement that it, in a manner, hath
   Declined your sovereignty of birth and spirit,   120
   How can ye turn your eyes off from that glass
   Wherein you may new trim and settle right
   A memorable name?
Thamasta.   The youth is idle.
Eroclea. Days, months, and years are passed since Menaphon
   Hath loved and served you truly. Menaphon,   125
   A man of no large distance in his blood
   From yours; in qualities desertful, graced
   With youth, experience, every happy gift
   That can by nature or by education
   Improve a gentleman. For him, great lady,   130
   Let me prevail, that you will yet at last
   Unlock the bounty which your love and care
   Have wisely treasured up, t'enrich his life.
Thamasta. Thou hast a moving eloquence; Parthenophill,
   Parthenophill, in vain we strive to cross   135
   The destiny that guides us. My great heart
   Is stooped so much beneath that wonted pride
   That first disguised it, that I now prefer
   A miserable life with thee before
   All other earthly comforts.
Eroclea.   Menaphon,   140
   By me, repeats the self-same words to you;
   You are too cruel if you can distrust
   His truth or my report.
Thamasta.   Go where thou wilt,
   I'll be an exile with thee; I will learn
   To bear all change of fortunes.
Eroclea.   For my friend   145

  120.] 'debased the supreme excellence of your birth and spirit', or 'debased the proud self-command proper to your birth and spirit'.
  121–3. *How . . . name*] 'new trim' and 'settle right' continue the image of the looking-glass into which one looks to make the best of one's appearance. By fixing her love on Menaphon (the glass) Thamasta will enhance her already memorable name and give herself properly in marriage.
  123. *idle*] foolish, out of his senses.
  126. *blood*] rank.

I plead with grounds of reason.
Thamasta.   For thy love,
  Hard-hearted youth, I here renounce all thoughts
  Of other hopes, of other entertainments——
Eroclea. Stay, as you honour virtue!
Thamasta.   When the proffers
  Of other greatness——
Eroclea.   Lady!
Thamasta.   When entreats   150
  Of friends——
Eroclea.   I'll ease your grief.
Thamasta.   Respect of kindred—
Eroclea. Pray give me hearing.
Thamasta.   Loss of fame—
Eroclea.   I crave
  But some few minutes.
Thamasta.   Shall infringe my vows,
  Let heaven——
Eroclea.   My love speaks t'ee; hear, then go on.
Thamasta. Thy love! Why 'tis a charm to stop a vow   155
  In its most violent course.
Eroclea.   Cupid has broke
  His arrows here and, like a child unarmed,
  Comes to make sport between us with no weapon
  But feathers stolen from his mother's doves.
Thamasta. This is mere trifling.
                        Lady, take a secret.   160
Eroclea.
  I am as you are—in a lower rank
  Else of the self-same sex—a maid, a virgin.
  And now, to use your own words, 'If your thoughts
  Censure me not with mercy, you may soon
  Conceive I have laid by that modesty   165
  Which should preserve a virtuous name unstained'.
Thamasta. Are you not mankind then?

154. speaks] *Weber;* speake *Q.*

---

146. *I . . . reason*] Her plea on behalf of Menaphon is rationally based whereas Thamasta's suit to her is the madness of passion.
148. *entertainments*] relationships.
159. *mother's doves*] The dove, symbol of mildness and concord, is often associated with Venus in literature and iconography.

Eroclea. When you shall read
　The story of my sorrows, with the change
　Of my misfortunes, in a letter printed
　From my unforged relation, I believe　　　　　　170
　You will not think the shedding of one tear
　A prodigality that misbecomes
　Your pity and my fortune.
Thamasta. Pray conceal
　The errors of my passions.
Eroclea. Would I had
　Much more of honour—as for life, I value't not—　175
　To venture on your secrecy.
Thamasta. It will be
　A hard task for my reason to relinquish
　The affection which was once devoted thine;
　I shall awhile repute thee still the youth
　I loved so dearly.
Eroclea. You shall find me ever　　　　180
　Your ready faithful servant.
Thamasta. O, the powers
　Who do direct our hearts laugh at our follies!
　We must not part yet.
Eroclea. Let not my unworthiness
　Alter your good opinion
Thamasta. I shall henceforth
　Be jealous of thy company with any;　　　　　185
　My fears are strong and many.

　　　　　　KALA *enters.*

Kala. Did your ladyship
　Call me?
Thamasta. For what?
Kala. Your servant, Menaphon,
　Desires admittance.

　　　　　　Enter MENAPHON.

---

174. passions] *Q;* passion *Dyce.*

169–70. *printed . . . relation*] recording my genuine account. 'Print': to commit to writing (*O.E.D.,* vb.4).
176. *venture*] presume.
187. *servant*] lover; cf. I.iii.62.

Menaphon. With your leave, great mistress,
I come——so private! Is this well, Parthenophill?
Eroclea. Sir, noble sir—
Menaphon. You are unkind and treacherous; 190
This 'tis to trust a straggler.
Thamasta. Prithee, servant—
Menaphon. I dare not question you; you are my mistress,
My prince's nearest kinswoman; but he——
Thamasta. Come, you are angry.
Menaphon. Henceforth I will bury
Unmanly passion in perpetual silence. 195
I'll court mine own distraction, dote on folly,
Creep to the mirth and madness of the age,
Rather than be so slaved again to woman
Which in her best of constancy is steadiest
In change and scorn.
Thamasta. How dare ye talk to me thus? 200
Menaphon. Dare! Were you not own sister to my friend,
Sister to my Amethus, I would hurl ye
As far off from mine eyes as from my heart,
For I would never more look on ye. Take
Your jewel t'ee. And, youth, keep under wing, 205
Or——boy——boy—
Thamasta. If commands be of no force,
Let me entreat thee, Menaphon.
Menaphon. 'Tis naught.
Fie, fie, Parthenophill, have I deserved
To be thus used?
Eroclea. I do protest——
Menaphon. You shall not;
Henceforth I will be free, and hate my bondage. 210

Enter AMETHUS.

Amethus. Away, away to court! The prince is pleased
To see a masque tonight; we must attend him.

199. steadiest] *Weber;* steddist *Q.*

---

196. *court . . . distraction*] seek to lose my senses.
197. *Creep*] cringe, abase myself.
205. *jewel*] i.e. Parthenophill.
207. *'tis naught*] Her entreaty is worthless; probable double sense, useless and not to be trusted (wicked).

108   THE LOVER'S MELANCHOLY   [ACT III

  'Tis near upon the time——How thrives your suit?
Menaphon. The judge, your sister, will decide it shortly.
Thamasta. Parthenophill, I will not trust you from me.   215
            [*Exeunt.*]

     Act III Scene iii

  Enter PALADOR, [SOPHRONOS,] ARETUS, CORAX
  with a paper plot, servants with torches.

Corax. Lights and attendance! I will show your highness
 A trifle of mine own brain. If you can,
 Imagine you were now in the university,
 You'll take it well enough; a scholar's fancy,
 A quab; 'tis nothing else, a very quab.   5
Palador. We will observe it.
Sophronos.   Yes, and grace it too, sir.
 For Corax else is humorous and testy.
Aretus. By any means; men singular in art
 Have always some odd whimsy more than usual.
Palador. The name of this conceit?
         Sir, it is called   10
Corax.
 The Masque of Melancholy.
Aretus.   We must look for
 Nothing but sadness here then.
Corax.   Madness rather,

215.1. *Exeunt*] Weber. 0.1. PALADOR] *Prince* Q. SOPHRONOS,] *Gifford.*

  0.2. *paper plot*] single-sheet playhouse document, essentially a list of entrances and exits for the guidance of actors, but also containing some stage directions and details of stage properties required. See Sir W. W. Greg, *Dramatic Documents from the Elizabethan Playhouses* (Oxford, 1931).
  5. *quab*] loosely defined in *O.E.D.* as several kinds of fish; for the figurative sense, 'a crude or shapeless thing', only this example from *The Lover's Melancholy* is cited (sb.1.1.2). Gifford also suggests 'an unfledged bird' in which sense 'the word is still used in that part of Devonshire where Ford was born'. That meaning is not given in *The English Dialect Dictionary*; 'quo(a)b' is recorded in dialect usage as 'bog', hence 'all of a quob', i.e. in a mess.
  7. *humorous*] moody.
  8. *singular in art*] distinguished in learning. For the relationship of this and the next line to Burton see Introduction, p. 8.
  12. *sadness*] The obsolete sense 'seriousness' is probably intended, although in this context 'mournfulness' would be appropriate.

SC III]   THE LOVER'S MELANCHOLY   109

 In several changes; melancholy is
The root as well of every apish frenzy,
Laughter and mirth, as dulness. Pray, my lord, 15
Hold and observe the plot; 'tis there expressed
In kind what shall be now expressed in action.

 Enter AMETHUS, MENAPHON, THAMASTA, EROCLEA [*as before*].

No interruption; take your places quickly.
Nay, nay, leave ceremony. Sound to the entrance!
            Flourish.

 Enter RHETIAS, *his face whited, black shag hair,*
  long nails, a piece of raw meat.

Rhetias. Bow, bow! wow, wow! the moon's eclipsed; I'll to the 20
churchyard and sup. Since I turned wolf, I bark and howl,
and dig up graves; I will never have the sun shine again;
'tis midnight, deep dark midnight. Get a prey and fall to—
I have catched thee now. Arre!
Corax. This kind is called Lycanthropia, sir, 25
When men conceive themselves wolves.
Palador.   Here I find it.

 Enter PELIAS. *A crown of feathers on, anticly rich.*

Pelias. I will hang 'em all, and burn my wife. Was I not an
emperor? My hand was kissed and ladies lay down before
me. In triumph did I ride with my nobles about me till the
mad dog bit me—I fell, and I fell, and I fell. It shall be 30
treason by statute for any man to name water, or wash his
hands, throughout all my dominions. Break all the

17.1. *as before*] This ed. 18. interruption] *Q corr.;* interpretation *Q uncorr.*

---

 17. *in kind*] in its essential nature.
 19.1. shag] matted, shaggy. The details of Rhetias' appearance may owe something to Burton, pp. 122–3; I: I: I: 4, where he describes a person afflicted with lycanthropia as 'of a pale, black, ugly, & fearful look'.
 20–5.] Burton, in the place referred to in the previous note, writes of the haunting of graves and churchyards at night.
 26.] Palador is following the 'plot' throughout the masque.
 26.1. anticly] grotesquely.
 29–30. *the . . . me*] Hydrophobia is another term for rabies.
 30–4. *It . . . whore*] Hatred of water and looking-glasses is associated by Burton with hydrophobia but he does not link sexual jealousy with the disease (pp. 123–4; I: I: I: 4).

110   THE LOVER'S MELANCHOLY   [ACT III

  looking-glasses, I will not see my horns. My wife cuckolds
  me; she is a whore, a whore, a whore, a whore!
Palador. Hydrophobia term you this?   35
Corax. And men possessed so shun all sight of water.
  Sometimes, if mixed with jealousy, it renders them
  Incurable, and oftentimes brings death.

   Enter PHILOSOPHER *in black rags, a copper chain on,*
    an old gown half off, and book.

Philosopher. Philosophers dwell in the moon. Speculation and
  theory girdle the world about like a wall. Ignorance, like 40
  an atheist, must be damned in the pit. I am very, very
  poor, and poverty is the physic for the soul; my opinions
  are pure and perfect. Envy is a monster, and I defy the
  beast.
Corax. Delirium this is called, which is mere dotage,   45
  Sprung from ambition first and singularity,
  Self-love and blind opinion of true merit.
Palador. I not dislike the course.

   Enter GRILLA *in a rich gown, great farthingale,*
    great ruff, muff, fan, and coxcomb on her head.

38.2. old . . . off] This detail seems to derive ultimately from a habit of Sir Thomas More recorded by Roger Ascham; he writes of a man who wished to be thought like More and so, like him, wore his gown 'awry upon the one shoulder' (*The Whole Works of Roger Ascham*, ed. Dr Giles (3 vols., London, 1865), III, 252–3). See also the following note with regard to the philosopher's costume.

39–47.] The delirium of the philosopher-scholar, with its marks of pride, poverty and self-conceit, is dealt with by Burton in 1: 2: 3: 14; 'like Diogenes, they brag inwardly, and feed themselves fat with a self-conceit of sanctity'. See also the following Subsection in Burton with its digression on the miseries of scholars where we are told that 'Poverty is the *Muse's* patrimony' (p. 266) and that a poor scholar wears 'an old torn gown, an ensign of his infelicity' (p. 264). Cf. also *The Pilgrimage to Parnassus*, l. 76, 'Learninge and pouertie will euer kiss' (*The Three Parnassus Plays*, ed. J. B. Leishman, London, 1949).

48.] The omission of the auxiliary 'do' before 'not' is often found at this period (Abbott, §305).

course] proceedings.

48.1–2. great . . . ruff] The absurdity of female pride is probably indicated in the dated costume. By the late sixteen-twenties only country women were wearing farthingales and the ruff was also being replaced for women by other kinds of neck and shoulder wear (Linthicum, pp. 161, 182).

coxcomb] professional fool's cap.

SC III]   THE LOVER'S MELANCHOLY   111

Grilla. Yes forsooth, and no forsooth—is not this fine? I pray
   your blessing, gaffer—here, here, here! Did he give me a   50
   shough, and cut off's tail!—Buss, buss, nuncle; and
   there's a pum for daddy.
Corax. You find this noted there, Phrenitis.
Palador.   True.
Corax. Pride is the ground on't; it reigns most in women.

   Enter CUCULUS *like a bedlam, singing.*

Cuculus. They that will learn to drink a health in hell   55
   Must learn on earth to take tobacco well,
   To take tobacco well, to take tobacco well;
   For in hell they drink nor wine, nor ale, nor beer,
   But fire, and smoke, and stench, as we do here.
Rhetias. I'll soop thee up.   60
Pelias. Thou'st straight to execution.
Grilla. Fool, fool, fool! Catch me and thou canst.
Philosopher. Expel him the house, 'tis a dunce.
Cuculus. Sings.   Hark! did ye not hear a rumbling?
            The goblins are now a tumbling;   65

55–9, 64–8, 75–86.] *Italics in Q.*

---

50. *gaffer*] term of respect for an elderly person.
51. *shough*] long-haired lap-dog.
Buss . . . nuncle] Kiss, kiss, uncle.
52. *pum*] presumably 'plum', a lisping pronunciation in keeping with the childish effect of the whole speech.
53–4.] Burton (p. 121; 1: 1: 1: 4) distinguishes phrenitis from other forms of melancholy as being accompanied by fever but does not connect it specifically with women or pride. Pride as a cause of melancholy is dealt with in 1: 2: 3: 14, but in connection with men only; the pride of women in adornment figures largely as a cause of love in men (3: 2: 2: 3) and has no relation to phrenitis in women.
54.1 *bedlam*] madman; cf. note to II.i.65.
56–9.] Although some writers defended its medicinal properties, from about 1600 onwards attacks on tobacco, both serious and jesting, proliferated and it was naturally and frequently associated with hell, as by Burton (p. 577; 2: 4: 2: 1) and by James I in the best-known of the attacks, *A Counterblaste to Tobacco* (1604). See William A. Penn, *The Soverane Herbe. A History of Tobacco* (London and New York, 1901), ch. XIII, for information on contemporary tobacco literature. Gifford notes that 'drinking tobacco' was the phrase used at the time but Ford's 'take tobacco' was certainly common usage.
60. *soop*] sweep.
61. *Thou'st*] thou wilt (Abbott, §461).

I'll tear 'em, I'll sear 'em,
I'll roar 'em, I'll gore 'em;
Now, now, now! My brains are a
    jumbling——
Bounce! the gun's off.

Palador. You name this here, Hypocondriacal. 70
Corax. Which is a windy flatuous humour stuffing
The head, and thence derived to th'animal parts.
To be too over-curious, loss of goods
Or friends, excess of fear or sorrows, cause it.

Enter a SEA-NYMPH *big-bellied, singing and dancing.*

Nymph.   Good your honours, 75
    Pray your worships,
    Dear your beauties,
Cuculus.   Hang thee!
    To lash your sides,
    To tame your hides, 80
    To scourge your prides,
    And bang thee.
Nymph. We're pretty and dainty, and I will begin;
See how they do jeer me, deride me, and grin.
Come sport me, come court me, your topsail advance, 85
And let us conclude our delights in a dance.
All. A dance, a dance, a dance!
Corax. This is the Wanton Melancholy; women
With child, possessed with this strange fury, often
Have danced three days together without ceasing. 90

---

69. *Bounce*] resounding thump; cf. I.i.11. Ewing, p. 40, note 30, says that 'bounce' is a cant word for breaking wind but I have been unable to verify this sense. Certainly 'windy flatuous humour' (l. 71) lends support to the idea.

70–4.] Burton describes hypochondria as a windy or flatuous melancholy (p. 323; 1: 2: 5: 4). He does not specifically link over-curiosity, loss of friends and goods to hypochondria, and Ford has taken these details from 1: 2: 4: 7 where Burton is discussing causes of melancholy in general.

74.1. *Sea-nymph*] This role would be appropriate to Kala although her presence in the preceding and succeeding scenes would not allow much time for change of costume.

80. *tame*] possibly a misprint for 'tanne', i.e. tan.

85. *topsail advance*] sail in full career.

88–90.] Burton (p. 124; 1: 1: 1: 4) describes St Vitus Dance ('the lascivious dance, Paracelsus calls it') and the feats of dancing performed by those afflicted. Burton does not say that the disease is peculiar to women but has

Palador. 'Tis very strange; but heaven is full of miracles.
The dance:——*which ended, they all run out in couples.*
Palador. We are thy debtor, Corax, for the gift
   Of this invention. But the plot deceives us;
   What means this empty space?
Corax   One kind of melancholy
   Is only left untouched; 'twas not in art   95
   To personate the shadow of that fancy.
   'Tis named Love Melancholy. As, for instance,
   Admit this stranger here—young man, stand forth—
   Entangled by the beauty of this lady,
   The great Thamasta, cherished in his heart   100
   The weight of hopes and fears, it were impossible
   To limn his passions in such lively colours
   As his own proper sufferance could express.
Eroclea. You are not modest, sir.
Thamasta.   Am I your mirth?
Corax. Love is the tyrant of the heart; it darkens   105
   Reason, confounds discretion; deaf to counsel,
   It runs a headlong course to desperate madness.
   O, were your highness but touched home, and throughly,
   With this—what shall I call it—devil——
Palador.   Hold!
   Let no man henceforth name the word again.   110
   Wait you my pleasure, youth. 'Tis late; to rest. [*Exit.*]
Corax. My lords——
Sophronos.   Enough; thou art a perfect arts-man.
Corax. Panthers may hide their heads, not change the skin;

111. *Exit*] Weber.

---

suggested Ford's big-bellied figure and 'Wanton Melancholy' in 'even great-bellied women sometimes (and yet never hurt their children) will dance so long that they can stir neither hand nor foot, but seem to be quite dead'. Ford may have presented the woman as a sea-nymph to render the figure less indelicate although, of course, mythological figures were common in court masques. Ford assimilated much from Shakespeare and the lady of *M.N.D.*, II.i.123–32, 'big-bellied' like the ships' sails, may have contributed to this figure.

   93. *invention*] device.
   96. *shadow*] image.
   98. *Admit*] suppose.
   103. *proper sufferance*] actual experience.
   104. *You . . . modest*] You offend against good taste.
   113.] The panther was supposed to prey on cattle by burying its fierce head

And love pent ne'er so close yet will be seen.   *Exeunt.*

114. *Exeunt*] Exeunt. / Finis actus Tertij. Q.

and attracting them by the pleasing scent and appearance of its skin (*The Excellent and Pleasant Worke of Julius Solinus Polyhistor*, trans. A. Golding (1587), O 1r).

114.] proverbial (Tilley, L 500).

Act IV

ACT IV SCENE i

Enter AMETHUS *and* MENAPHON.

Amethus. Dote on a stranger?
Menaphon.   Court him, plead, and sue to him.
Amethus. Affectionately?
Menaphon.   Servilely; and pardon me
 If I say basely.
Amethus.   Women in their passions
 Like false fires flash to fright our trembling senses,
 Yet in themselves contain nor light nor heat.   5
 My sister do this? She, whose pride did scorn
 All thoughts that were not busied on a crown,
 To fall so far beneath her fortunes now?
 You are my friend.
Menaphon.   What I confirm is truth.
Amethus. Truth, Menaphon?
       If I conceived you were   10
Menaphon.
 Jealous of my sincerity and plainness,
 Then, sir——
Amethus.   What then sir?
Menaphon.   I would then resolve
 You were as changeable in vows of friendship
 As is Thamasta in her choice of love.

Act IV] Actus IIII. Scena I. *Q.*

4–5.] False fire was (1) the blank discharge of firearms; (2) inflammable material used in fireworks. Ford is making a distinction between the outward show of women's passions and their lack of real substance, but the simile seems inexact since false fire would produce considerable light even if little heat.
 11. *Jealous*] suspicious.

    That sin is double, running in a blood, 15
    Which justifies another being worse.
Amethus. My Menaphon, excuse me; I grow wild
    And would not willingly believe the truth
    Of my dishonour. She shall know how much
    I am a debtor to thy noble goodness 20
    By checking the contempt her poor desires
    Have sunk her fame in. Prithee, tell me, friend,
    How did the youth receive her?
Menaphon. With a coldness
    As modest and as hopeless as the trust
    I did repose in him could wish or merit. 25
Amethus. I will esteem him dearly.

Enter THAMASTA *and* KALA.

Menaphon. Sir, your sister.
Thamasta. Servant, I have employment for ye.
Amethus. Hark ye;
    The mask of your ambition is fallen off;
    Your pride hath stooped to such an abject lowness
    That you have now discovered to report 30
    Your nakedness in virtue, honours, shame——
Thamasta. You are turned satire.
Amethus. All the flatteries
    Of greatness have exposed ye to contempt.
Thamasta. This is mere railing.
Amethus. You have sold your birth

26.1.] Dyce; *after l. 25* Q.

15–16.] 'running in a blood' is equivalent to modern 'running in the blood', i.e. characteristic of a family. The syntax of the two lines appears to be confused; the referent of 'running in a blood' is 'sin' not 'double sin', since the latter does not apply to Thamasta. I take Menaphon's sense to be that the sin of broken faith is characteristic of Amethus' family but that his sin is twice that of Thamasta, and worse, in justifying her sin.

22. *fame*] reputation.

27. *Servant . . . ye*] Thamasta, having learned of the true identity of Parthenophill (by the letter referred to at III.ii.169), wishes Menaphon to convey to Cleophila a letter disclosing the happy news; balked in this intention, she uses Cuculus as messenger (IV.ii.176ff.).

30. *discovered . . . report*] disclosed to be talked about.

32. *satire*] satirist.

32–3. *flatteries of greatness*] delusions attendant on high position; or, possibly, self-indulgencies enjoyed by the great.

SC I]   THE LOVER'S MELANCHOLY   117

  For lust.
Thamasta. Lust!
Amethus.   Yes, and at a dear expense   35
  Purchased the only glories of a wanton.
Thamasta. A wanton!
Amethus.   Let repentance stop your mouth;
  Learn to redeem your fault.
Kala. [*Aside to Menaphon.*] I hope your tongue
  Has not betrayed my honesty.
Menaphon. [*Aside to Kala.*] Fear nothing.
Thamasta. If, Menaphon, I hitherto have strove 40
  To keep a wary guard about my fame;
  If I have used a woman's skill to sift
  The constancy of your protested love,
  You cannot, in the justice of your judgement,
  Impute that to a coyness or neglect   45
  Which my discretion and your service aimed
  For noble purposes.
Menaphon.   Great mistress, no.
  I rather quarrel with mine own ambition,
  That durst to soar so high as to feed hope
  Of any least desert that might entitle   50
  My duty to a pension from your favours.
Amethus. And therefore, lady—pray, observe him well—
  He henceforth covets plain equality,
  Endeavouring to rank his fortunes low
  With some fit partner whom, without presumption, 55
  Without offence or danger, he may cherish,
  Yes and command too, as a wife—a wife,
  A wife, my most great lady!
Kala. [*Aside.*]   All will out.
Thamasta. Now I perceive the league of amity,
  Which you have long between ye vowed and kept, 60
  Is sacred and inviolable; secrets

38. *Aside to Menaphon*] So Weber. 39. *Aside to Kala*] So Dyce. 53. equality] *Q corr.;* equally *Q uncorr.* 58. *Aside*] Weber.

---

 50. *Of . . . desert*] arising from any small merit he might possess.
 51. *pension*] wages. In using this term Menaphon seems to have divested the courtly servant/mistress relationship of its glamour which would incline one to think that this whole speech is sarcastic in its self-abasement.

Of every nature are in common t'ee.
I have trespassed, and I have been faulty.
Let not too rude a censure doom me guilty,
Or judge my error wilful without pardon. 65
Menaphon. Gracious and virtuous mistress!
Amethus. 'Tis a trick;
There is no trust in female cunning, friend,
Let her first purge her follies past, and clear
The wrong done to her honour, by some sure
Apparent testimony of her constancy, 70
Or we will not believe these childish plots.
As you respect my friendship lend no ear
To a reply. Think on't.
Menaphon. Pray, love your fame.
Exeunt MENAPHON, AMETHUS.
Thamasta. Gone! I am sure awaked. Kala, I find
You have not been so trusty as the duty 75
You owed required.
Kala. Not I? I do protest
I have been, madam.
Thamasta. Be no matter what,
I'm paid in mine own coin. Something I must,
And speedily——So!——Seek out Cuculus,
Bid him attend me instantly.
Kala. That antic! 80
The trim old youth shall wait ye.
Thamasta. Wounds may be mortal which are wounds indeed,
But no wounds deadly till our honours bleed. *Exeunt.*

---

71. *childish plots*] Thamasta's unconvincing (to Amethus) excusing of her conduct.

78. *I'm ... coin*] I take the primary sense to be that she is getting from Menaphon and Amethus a taste of the pride she had shown them; her mistaken passion for Parthenophill may also be referred to—that was unrequited, a punishment for her rejection of Menaphon's love.

81. *wait ye*] wait on you.

82-3.] This probably derives from the proverbial 'An ill wound is cured, not an ill name' (Tilley, W 928) although the first citation given by Tilley is 1640. Double inverted commas in Q at the beginning of l. 83 indicate a sententia.

Act IV Scene ii

Enter RHETIAS *and* CORAX.

Rhetias. Thou'rt an excellent fellow. Diabolo! O these lousy
close-stool empirics that will undertake all cures yet know
not the causes of any diseases. Dog-leeches! By the four
elements, I honour thee; could find in my heart to turn
knave and be thy flatterer. 5
Corax. Sirrah, 'tis pity thou'st not been a scholar;
Thou'rt honest, blunt, and rude enough, o' conscience.
But for thy lord, now, I have put him to't.
Rhetias. He chafes hugely, fumes like a stew-pot. Is he not
monstrously overgone in frenzy? 10
Corax. Rhetias, 'tis not a madness, but his sorrow's
Close-griping grief and anguish of the soul
That torture him; he carries hell on earth
Within his bosom. 'Twas a prince's tyranny
Caused his distraction, and a prince's sweetness 15
Must qualify that tempest of his mind.
Rhetias. Corax, to praise thy art were to assure
The misbelieving world that the sun shines
When 'tis in th'full meridian of his beauty;
No cloud of black detraction can eclipse 20
The light of thy rare knowledge. Henceforth, casting
All poor disguises off that play in rudeness,
Call me your servant; only for the present,
I wish a happy blessing to your labours.
Heaven crown your undertakings! And, believe me, 25
Ere many hours can pass, at our next meeting,

1. these] *Weber;* this *Q.*   2. empirics] *Weber;* Empricks *Q.*   6. thou'st] *Dyce;*
th'ast *Q.*

---

1. *Diabolo*] devil.
2. *close-stool*] commode.
3. *Dog-leeches*] veterinary practitioners; so also horse-leech, bullock-leech
etc. Cf. bear-leech, V.ii.19.
6. *thou'st*] thou hadst; archaic form of 'had'.
8. *thy lord*] i.e. Meleander.
14–16. *'Twas . . . mind*] The first prince is Palador's father and the second
Palador himself; 'qualify': calm.
19. *in . . . meridian*] at the highest altitude, noon.
22. *play in rudeness*] act an uncivil role; the acting metaphor continues from
'disguises'. Rhetias is relinquishing his role of malcontent.

The bonds my duty owes shall be full cancelled.   *Exit.*
Corax. Farewell——A shrewd-brain whoreson; there's pith
   In his untoward plainness——

   Enter TROLLIO *with a murrion on.*

                    Now, the news?
Trollio. Worshipful master doctor, I have a great deal of I   30
   cannot tell what to say t'ee. My lord thunders; every word
   that comes out of his mouth roars like a cannon. The
   house shook once; my young lady dares not be seen.
Corax. We will roar with him, Trollio, if he roar.
Trollio. He has got a great pole-axe in his hand, and fences 35
   it up and down the house as if he were to make room for
   the pageants. I have provided me a murrion for fear of a
   clap on the coxcomb.
Corax. No matter for the murrion, here's my cap;
   Thus will I pull it down, and thus outstare him.   40
                    [*Puts on a Gorgon mask.*]
Trollio. [*Aside.*] The physician is got as mad as my lord——
   [*To him.*] O brave! a man of worship.
Corax. Let him come, Trollio; I will firk his trangdido,
   And bounce and bounce in metal, honest Trollio.
Trollio. [*Aside.*] He vapours like a tinker, and struts like a 45

40.1. *Puts on a Gorgon mask*] *Gifford subst.*   41. *Aside*] *So Dyce.*   42. *To him*]
This ed.   45. *Aside*] *Gifford.*

27.] This refers to either the service he has just pledged to Corax or his duty
to his master, Meleander.
   28–9. *there's . . . plainness*] There's a gravity of purpose behind his perverse
and blunt behaviour.
   29.1 murrion] helmet.
   35–7. *He . . . pageants*] Meleander is being likened to a whiffler, an armed
official employed to clear the way for processions or public spectacles.
   40.1. Gorgon] See note to ll. 53–4 below.
   42. *of worship*] to be honoured.
   43. *I . . . trangdido*] 'firk' could certainly mean 'strike' (cf. *Lady's Trial*,
II.ii; vol. III, 38, 'he has firk'd / And mumbled the rogue Turks'), and Weber
suggests, 'I will strike his pole-axe out of his hand', but this is not convincing.
The Fancies has 'tickle their trangdidos' (IV.i; vol. II, 292), where the context
suggests that 'trangdido' means 'backside' since the speaker, Secco, is
flourishing a rod, intent on beating the page, Nitido. This offers a meaning for
'firk his trangdido', and both phrases may be variations of 'tickle your
catastrophe' (*2 H 4*, II.i.57–8), i.e. 'make your backside tingle'.
   44. *bounce . . . metal*] bluster courageously.
   45.] Tinkers were often identified with gipsies, itinerant beggars and

SC II]   THE LOVER'S MELANCHOLY   121

   juggler.
Meleander. Within. So-ho, so-ho!
Trollio. There, there, there! Look to your right worshipful,
  look to yourself.
     Enter MELEANDER *with a pole-axe.*
Meleander. Show me the dog whose triple-throated noise   50
  Hath roused a lion from his uncouth den
  To tear the cur in pieces.
Corax.   Stay thy paws,
  Courageous beast; else, lo! the Gorgon's skull
  That shall transform thee to that restless stone
  Which Sisyphus rolls up against the hill,   55
  Whence, tumbling down again, it with his weight
  Shall crush thy bones and puff thee into air.
Meleander. Hold, hold thy conquering breath; 'tis stronger far
  Than gunpowder and garlic. If the fates
  Have spun my thread and my spent clew of life   60
  Be now untwisted, let us part like friends.
  Lay up my weapon, Trollio, and be gone.
Trollio. Yes, sir, with all my heart.
       Exit TROLLIO [*with the pole-axe*].
Meleander.   This friend and I
  Will walk, and gabble wisely.

47. Meleander] *Menander Q.* 53. Gorgon's] *Gifford; gorgeous Q.* 63. heart.] heart.—— *Q.* *with the pole-axe*] *So Gifford.*

---

performers; jugglers were similarly regarded with contempt and suspicion; 'vapours': brags.
 47. *So-ho*] hunting cry.
 50–2. *Show ... pieces*] The dog is the three-headed Cerberus, guardian of Hades, whom Hercules (the lion) had to capture as one of his twelve labours; Hercules wore the skin of the Nemean lion whom he slew as another of his labours.
 51. *uncouth*] wild.
 53–4. *Gorgon's ... thee*] The three Gorgons were monstrous women whose gaze turned anything to stone. Corax is wearing a Gorgon mask.
 54–5. *restless ... hill*] Sisyphus, legendary king of Corinth, was condemned to this punishment in Hades; the stone is 'restless' because it always rolled back after having been pushed to the summit.
 59–61. *fates ... untwisted*] The three Fates, Clotho, Lachesis and Atropos, decreed a man's span of life, and were represented as spinning from a distaff the allotted thread (span); 'clew': a ball of thread.

Corax.   I allow
    The motion. [*Takes off his mask.*] On!
Meleander.   So politicians thrive,   65
    That with their crabbèd faces and sly tricks,
    Legerdemain, ducks, cringes, formal beards,
    Crisped hairs, and punctual cheats, do wriggle in
    Their heads first, like a fox, to rooms of state,
    Then the whole body follows.
Corax.   Then they fill   70
    Lordships, steal women's hearts; with them and theirs
    The world runs round; yet these are square men still.
Meleander. There are none poor but such as engross offices.
Corax. None wise but unthrifts, bankrupts, beggars, rascals.
Meleander. The hangman is a rare physician.   75
Corax. [*Aside.*] That's not so good. [*To him.*] It shall be
    granted.
Meleander. All the buzz of drugs and minerals and simples,
    Blood-lettings, vomits, purges, or what else
    Is conjured up by men of art to gull
    Liege-people and rear golden piles, are trash   80
    To a strong well-wrought halter; there the gout,
    The stone, yes, and the melancholy devil,
    Are cured in less time than a pair of minutes.
    Build me a gallows in this very plot
    And I'll dispatch your business.
Corax.   Fix the knot   85
    Right under the left ear.
Meleander.   Sirrah, make ready.
Corax. Yet do not be too sudden; grant me leave
    To give a farewell to a creature long
    Absented from me. 'Tis a daughter, sir,
    Snatched from me in her youth, a handsome girl;   90

---

65. *Takes off his mask*] So Gifford.   68–70.] *Weber; prose in* Q.   76. *Aside*] Gifford.   *To him*] This ed.   81. strong well-wrought] *Gifford;* well-strong-wrought Q.

64–5. *I . . . motion*] I agree to the proposal.
68. *punctual cheats*] ceremonious deceptions.
68–70. *wriggle . . . follows*] proverbial (Tilley, F 655).
72. *square*] honest.
73. *engross*] monopolise.
77. *buzz*] busy talk.
simples] medicinal herbs.

   She comes to ask a blessing.
Meleander.   Pray, where is she?
   I cannot see her yet.
Corax.   She makes more haste
   In her quick prayers than her trembling steps,
   Which many griefs have weakened.
Meleander.   Cruel man!
   How canst thou rip a heart that's cleft already   95
   With injuries of time? Whilst I am frantic,
   Whilst throngs of rude divisions huddle on,
   And do disrank my brains from peace and sleep,
   So long I am insensible of cares.
   As balls of wild-fire may be safely touched,   100
   Not violently sundered and thrown up,
   So my distempered thoughts rest in their rage,
   Not hurried in the air of repetition
   Or memory of my misfortunes past.
   Then are my griefs struck home when they are reclaimed   105
   To their own pity of themselves——Proceed;
   What of your daughter now?
Corax.   I cannot tell ye,
   'Tis now out of my head again; my brains
   Are crazy; I have scarce slept one sound sleep
   These twelve months.
Meleander.   'Las, poor man! canst thou imagine   110
   To prosper in the task thou tak'st in hand
   By practising a cure upon my weakness,
   And yet be no physician for thyself?
   Go, go, turn over all thy books once more
   And learn to thrive in modesty, for impudence   115
   Does least become a scholar. Thou art a fool,
   A kind of learnèd fool.
Corax.   I do confess it.
Meleander. If thou canst wake with me, forget to eat,

105.] *Weber;* two lines in *Q* . . . home, / . . . reclaym'd,

 93. *prayers*] dissyllabic.
 100–1.] Wildfire was an incendiary substance used in warfare, projected in pots or tubs; such pots would be already burning on projection so Ford may be referring to cast-iron shells stuffed with wildfire and furnished with a fuse, thus exploding in the air or on impact ('violently sundered').
 118. *wake*] continue unsleeping.

>   Renounce the thought of greatness, tread on fate,
>   Sigh out a lamentable tale of things   120
>   Done long ago, and ill done; and, when sighs
>   Are wearied, piece up what remains behind
>   With weeping eyes, and hearts that bleed to death,
>   Thou shalt be a companion fit for me,
>   And we will sit together like true friends   125
>   And never be divided. With what greediness
>   Do I hug my afflictions! There's no mirth
>   Which is not truly seasoned with some madness:
>   As, for example——   *Exit.*
>
> *Corax.*   What new crotchet next?
>   There is so much sense in this wild distraction   130
>   That I am almost out of my wits too,
>   To see and hear him; some few hours more
>   Spent here would turn me apish, if not frantic.
>
>   *Enter* MELEANDER *and* CLEOPHILA.
>
> *Meleander.* In all the volumes thou hast turned, thou man
>   Of knowledge, hast thou met with any rarity   135
>   Worthy thy contemplation like to this?
>   The model of the heavens, the earth, the waters,
>   The harmony and sweet consent of times,
>   Are not of such an excellence, in form
>   Of their creation, as the infinite wonder   140
>   That dwells within the compass of this face.
>   And yet I tell thee, scholar, under this
>   Well-ordered sign is lodged such an obedience
>   As will hereafter, in another age,
>   Strike all comparison into a silence.   145
>   She had a sister too; but as for her,
>   If I were given to talk, I could describe
>   A pretty piece of goodness; let that pass——

---

122. *piece . . . behind*] eke out our remaining grief.

137–8.] The idea of the cosmic harmony is of Greek origin and is frequently found in the literature of the period. Cf. E. M. W. Tillyard, *The Elizabethan World Picture* (London, 1943), pp. 94–9.

model] The sense here required is 'system' but *O.E.D.*, sb.II.7.b only records this sense for immaterial things, institutions.

consent] concent (concord, harmony); frequently spelt consent.

143. *Well-ordered sign*] sign of the zodiac; an astrological metaphor in which Cleophila is thought of as a sign conferring obedience.

SC II]   THE LOVER'S MELANCHOLY   125

    We must be wise sometimes. What would you with her?
Corax. I with her? Nothing, by your leave, sir, I;   150
    It is not my profession.
Meleander.   You are saucy,
    And, as I take it, scurvy in your sauciness,
    To use no more respect——Good soul, be patient,
    We are a pair of things the world doth laugh at.
    Yet be content, Cleophila; those clouds   155
    Which bar the sun from shining on our miseries
    Will never be chased off till I am dead,
    And then some charitable soul will take thee
    Into protection. I am hasting on;
    The time cannot be long.
Cleophila.   I do beseech ye,   160
    Sir, as you love your health, as you respect
    My safety, let not passion overrule you.
Meleander. It shall not; I am friends with all the world.
    Get me some wine; to witness that I will be
    An absolute good fellow I will drink with thee.   165
Corax. [*Aside to Cleophila.*] Have you prepared his cup?
Cleophila. [*Aside to Corax.*]   'Tis in readiness.

        Enter CUCULUS *and* GRILLA.

Cuculus. By your leave, gallants, I come to speak with a young
    lady, as they say, the old Trojan's daughter of the house.
Meleander. Your business with my lady daughter, toss-pot?
Grilla. Toss-pot! O base! Toss-pot!   170
Cuculus. [*Aside to Grilla.*] Peace! Dost not see in what case he
    is? [*To Meleander.*] I would do my own commendations to
    her, that's all.
Meleander. Do. Come, my genius, we will quaff in wine
    Till we grow wise.
Corax.   True nectar is divine.   175

166. *Aside to Cleophila*] So Gifford.   *Aside to Corax*] So Dyce.   171. *Aside to Grilla*] This ed.   172. *To Meleander*] This ed.

---

  151. *profession*] of pimp, procurer.
  168. *Trojan*] boon companion; a cant term.
  169. *toss-pot*] drunkard.
  174. *genius*] tutelary spirit.
  175. *True . . . divine*] literally so because nectar is the drink of the gods, but Corax also intends the metaphorical sense of nectar, i.e. wisdom, following on

126   THE LOVER'S MELANCHOLY   [ACT IV

Exeunt MELEANDER *and* CORAX.

Cuculus. So; I am glad he is gone. Page, walk aside. Sweet beauty, I am sent ambassador from the mistress of my thoughts, to you, the mistress of my desires.

Cleophila. So, sir, I pray be brief.

Cuculus. That you may know I am not, as they say, an animal, 180 which is, as they say, a kind of cokes, which is, as the learned term, an ass, a puppy, a widgeon, a dolt, a noddy, a ——

Cleophila. As you please.

Cuculus. Pardon me for that, it shall be as you please indeed. 185 Forsooth, I love to be courtly and in fashion.

Cleophila. Well, to your embassy; what, or from whom?

Cuculus. Marry, what is more than I know; for to know what's what, is to know what's what and for what's what. But these are foolish figures and to little purpose. 190

Cleophila. From whom, then, are you sent?

Cuculus. There you come to me again. O, to be in the favour of great ladies is as much to say as to be great in ladies' favours.

Cleophila. Good time a' day t'ee; I can stay no longer. 195

Cuculus. By this light, but you must, for now I come to't. The most excellent, most wise, most dainty, precious, loving, kind, sweet, intolerably fair lady Thamasta commends to your little hands this letter of importance. By your leave, let me first kiss, and then deliver it in fashion to your own 200 proper beauty.

Cleophila. To me from her? 'Tis strange; I dare peruse it.

Cuculus. Good. [*Aside.*] O that I had not resolved to live a single life! Here's temptation able to conjure up a spirit with a witness. So, so; she has read it. 205

Cleophila. Is't possible? Heaven, thou art great and bountiful. Sir, I much thank your pains; and to the princess

175.1. *Exeunt*] *Weber; Exit Q.*   203. *Aside*] *Dyce.*

---

from Meleander's association of wine and wisdom. Cf. Jonson's *Poetaster*, V.i.88–9, 'But knowledge is the *nectar*, that keepes sweet / A perfect soule'.

181–2. *cokes . . . widgeon . . . noddy*] all terms for 'simpleton'. A widgeon is a wild duck, formerly supposed stupid.

190. *figures*] figures of speech, verbal quibbles.

204. *conjure . . . spirit*] sexual innuendo; the temptation of Cleophila's beauty is such as to raise up his 'spirit'. Cf. *Rom.*, II.i.23–6.

205. *with a witness*] most emphatically.

SC III]   THE LOVER'S MELANCHOLY   127

  Let my love, duty, service, be remembered.
Cuculus. They shall, mad-dame.
Cleophila. When we of hopes or helps are quite bereaven, 210
  Our humble prayers have entrance into heaven.
Cuculus. That's my opinion clearly and without doubt.
             Exeunt.

ACT IV   SCENE iii

Enter ARETUS *and* SOPHRONOS.

Aretus. The prince is throughly moved.
Sophronos.   I never saw him
  So much distempered.
Aretus.   What should this young man be,
  Or whither can he be conveyed?
Sophronos.   'Tis to me
  A mystery; I understand it not.
Aretus.   Nor I.

Enter PALADOR, AMETHUS, *and* PELIAS.

Palador. Ye have consented all to work upon 5
  The softness of my nature; but take heed:
  Though I can sleep in silence, and look on
  The mockery ye make of my dull patience,
  Yet 'ee shall know, the best of ye, that in me
  There is a masculine, a stirring spirit, 10
  Which provoked, shall like a bearded comet
  Set ye at gaze, and threaten horror.
Pelias.   Good sir—
Palador. Good sir! 'Tis not your active wit or language,
  Nor your grave politic wisdoms, lords, shall dare
  To checkmate and control my just commands. 15

Enter MENAPHON.

  Where is the youth, your friend? Is he found yet?

212.1. *Exeunt*] Weber; *Exit* Q. 4.1. PALADOR] *Prince* Q.

---

 209. *mad-dame*] thus in Q, indicating the pun.
 210. *bereaven*] bereft; archaic form.

 5. *consented all*] agreed between yourselves.
 11. *bearded comet*] comet with a 'tail'; comets were regarded as evil omens.

Menaphon. Not to be heard of.
Palador.   Fly then to the desert
  Where thou didst first encounter this fantastic,
  This airy apparition. Come no more
  In sight; get ye all from me; he that stays   20
  Is not my friend.
Amethus.   'Tis strange.
Aretus.   ⎱
Sophronos.   ⎰   We must obey.
                               Exeunt all but PALADOR.
Palador. Some angry power cheats with rare delusions
  My credulous sense; the very soul of reason
  Is troubled in me——The physician
  Presented a strange masque, the view of it   25
  Puzzled my understanding; but the boy——

                    Enter RHETIAS.

  Rhetias, thou art acquainted with my griefs;
  Parthenophill is lost and I would see him,
  For he is like to something I remember
  A great while since, a long, long time ago.   30
Rhetias. I have been diligent, sir, to pry into every corner for
  discovery, but cannot meet with him. There is some trick,
  I am confident.
Palador. There is; there is some practice, sleight or plot.
Rhetias. I have apprehended a fair wench in an odd private   35
  lodging in the city, as like the youth in face as can by
  possibility be discerned.

21.1. PALADOR] *the Prince* Q.   35–7.] *Weber; verse in* Q . . . odde / . . . Youth / . . . discern'd.

---

18. *fantastic*] either (1) an adjective, 'fabulous', 'unreal' (*O.E.D.*, a.1), qualifying 'apparition'; or (2) a noun, 'a person given to fanciful ideas or showy dress' (*O.E.D.*, sb.1, 2), although these senses seem not appropriate here.

19. *apparition*] phenomenon, or appearance of a remarkable kind (*O.E.D.*, 8). For the possible sense, 'sham', 'illusion', cf. *Perkin Warbeck*, IV.iii.13 (ed. Peter Ure, 1968).

22–4. *Some . . . me*] Contemporary psychology divided the soul of man into three sub-souls, the vegetative, the sensitive and the rational (see Babb, pp. 2–5). Palador's sensitive soul is deceived, but worse, his rational soul, ultimate commander of the vegetative and sensitive souls, is bewildered.

36–7. *by possibility*] that can possibly; cf. V.i.85; 'by': according to (Abbott, §145).

Palador. How, Rhetias!

Rhetias. If it be not Parthenophill in long coats, 'tis a spirit in
    his likeness; answer I can get none from her; you shall see   40
    her.

Palador. The young man in disguise, upon my life,
    To steal out of the land.

Rhetias.   I'll send him t'ee. *Exit* RHETIAS.

Palador. Do, do, my Rhetias.

    Enter EROCLEA *in woman's attire, and listens.*

            As there is by nature
    In everything created contrariety,   45
    So likewise is there unity and league
    Between them in their kind; but man, the abstract
    Of all perfection, which the workmanship
    Of heaven hath modelled, in himself contains
    Passions of several quality; the music   50
    Of man's fair composition best accords
    When 'tis in consort, not in single strains.
    My heart has been untuned these many months

39–41.] *Weber; verse in Q . . . coates, | . . . answer | . . . her.* 44.1.] *This ed.; after l. 43 Q.*

44–7. *As . . . kind*] I cannot gloss these lines with any confidence. Perhaps, 'Although each created thing is made up of contrary or heterogeneous elements these are unified and harmonized for each kind.' This makes the required contrast with the condition of man described in the following lines as one of various passions still needing to be united in harmony. E. A. J. Honigmann suggests, 'As there is contrariety by nature in everything created, so likewise is there uniformity of substance (*O.E.D.*, unity 1.II.6; one citation, 1638) and accord between created things of one kind.' This is perhaps the more natural reading but since, in this interpretation, the harmony is between individuals of the same species it seems not to make such an effective contrast with the condition of man where the harmony is wanting within the individual.

47. *abstract*] compendium.

49–51. *in . . . composition*] The idea behind this musical metaphor is the Boethian *musica humana*, the tempering of the various parts of body and soul, and parallel to the *musica mundana* referred to at IV.ii.137–8. Boethian ideas on music were influential well into the sixteenth century. See John Hollander, *The Untuning of the Sky* (Princeton, 1961), pp. 24–5.

52.] The metaphor does not continue very happily from the preceding lines since the concept of man as composed of various passions has changed into 'single strain' to maintain the antithesis with 'consort' and connect with the following lines.

53–5. *My . . . consisted*] The 'tuning' of his heart is to be effected by love

   Wanting her presence, in whose equal love
   True harmony consisted. Living here   55
   We are heaven's bounty all, but fortune's exercise.
Eroclea. Minutes are numbered by the fall of sands,
   As by an hour-glass; the span of time
   Doth waste us to our graves, and we look on it.
   An age of pleasures, revelled out, comes home   60
   At last and ends in sorrow; but the life
   Weary of riot numbers every sand,
   Wailing in sighs, until the last drop down,
   So to conclude calamity in rest.
Palador. What echo yields a voice to my complaints? 65
   Can I be nowhere private?
Eroclea. [*Coming forward.*] Let the substance
   As suddenly be hurried from your eyes
   As the vain sound can pass your ear,
   If no impression of a troth vowed yours   *Kneels.*
   Retains a constant memory.
Palador.   Stand up;   70
   'Tis not the figure stamped upon thy cheeks,
   The cozenage of thy beauty, grace, or tongue,
   Can draw from me a secret that hath been
   The only jewel of my speechless thoughts.
Eroclea. I am so worn away with fears and sorrows,   75
   So wintered with the tempests of affliction,
   That the bright sun of your life-quick'ning presence
   Hath scarce one beam of force to warm again
   That spring of cheerful comfort which youth once

57–8. sands, / As by an hour-glass; the] *Weber;* Sands; / As by an houre-glasse, / the *Q.* 66. *Coming forward*] *comes forward, and kneels Gifford.* 68. pass] *Q;* pass, sir, from *Gifford.*

('equal love': answering to his own in quality). On the association of love and music at the time see Gretchen L. Finney, *Musical Backgrounds for English Literature: 1580–1650* (New Brunswick, 1961), ch. IV.
 56.] We are all the gift of God but subject to the caprice of fortune.
 59. *and . . . it*] 'it' could refer to 'hour-glass' but then the sense seems lame. Perhaps the reference is to the whole clause, 'the span . . . graves', and the meaning, 'and we are (helpless) lookers-on'; or, taking 'and' to mean 'if' (Abbott, 101), 'if we consider the matter'.
 71–2.] coinage metaphor, the 'figure' being the image of the monarch stamped on the coin; Palador implies that she is counterfeit coin and that her face is not that of the true Eroclea.

  Apparelled in fresh looks.
Palador.   Cunning imposter!   80
  Untruth hath made thee subtle in thy trade.
  If any neighbouring greatness hath seduced
  A free-born resolution to attempt
  Some bolder act of treachery by cutting
  My weary days off, wherefore, cruel mercy,   85
  Hast thou assumed a shape that would make treason
  A piety, guilt pardonable, bloodshed
  As holy as the sacrifice of peace?
Eroclea. The incense of my love-desires are flamed
  Upon an altar of more constant proof.   90
  Sir, O sir, turn me back into the world,
  Command me to forget my name, my birth,
  My father's sadness, and my death alive,
  If all remembrance of my faith hath found
  A burial without pity in your scorn.   95
Palador. My scorn, disdainful boy, shall soon unweave
  The web thy art hath twisted. Cast thy shape off,
  Disrobe the mantle of a feignèd sex,
  And so I may be gentle; as thou art
  There's witchcraft in thy language, in thy face,   100
  In thy demeanours. Turn, turn from me, prithee,
  For my belief is armed else. Yet, fair subtlety,
  Before we part—for part we must—be true;
  Tell me thy country.
Eroclea.   Cyprus.
Palador.   Ha! Thy father?
Eroclea. Meleander.
Palador.   Hast a name?
Eroclea.   A name of misery,   105

---

85. *cruel mercy*] (*Cruell-mercy*) Q.

 82. *greatness*] state.
 82–3. *seduced ... resolution*] precise sense unclear; 'seduced an unconstrained resolve (to be loyal)', or 'seduced a resolution born free (of treachery)'.
 85. *cruel mercy*] vocative addressed to Eroclea. See collation.
 89.] 'are' should agree with 'incense' not 'love-desires'.
 90. *of . . . proof*] that will prove more constant (than to be guilty of the crime of which you accuse me).
 102. *For . . . else*] Palador seems to mean, 'for otherwise what I believe about you will turn to aggression'.

        The unfortunate Eroclea.
Palador.   There is danger
        In this seducing counterfeit. Great goodness,
        Hath honesty and virtue left the time?
        Are we become so impious that to tread
        The path of impudence is law and justice?   110
        Thou vizard of a beauty ever sacred,
        Give me thy name.
Eroclea.   Whilst I was lost to memory
        Parthenophill did shroud my shame in change
        Of sundry rare misfortunes; but since now
        I am, before I die, returned to claim   115
        A convoy to my grave, I must not blush
        To let Prince Palador, if I offend,
        Know when he dooms me, that he dooms Eroclea.
        I am that woeful maid.
Palador.   Join not too fast
        Thy penance with the story of my suff'rings.   120
        So dwelt simplicity with virgin truth,
        So martyrdom and holiness are twins,
        As innocence and sweetness on thy tongue.
        But let me by degrees collect my senses;
        I may abuse my trust. Tell me, what air   125
        Hast thou perfumed since tyranny first ravished
        The contract of our hearts?
Eroclea.   Dear sir, in Athens
        Have I been buried.
Palador.   Buried! Right, as I
        In Cyprus——Come to trial: if thou beest
        Eroclea, in my bosom I can find thee.   130
Eroclea. As I Prince Palador in mine; this gift
                              She shows him a tablet.
        His bounty blest me with, the only physic
        My solitary cares have hourly took
        To keep me from despair.
Palador.   We are but fools

---

111. *vizard*] mask.
116. *convoy*] funeral train.
125. *I . . . trust*] I may be mistaken to trust you.
130. *thee*] the miniature referred to at II.i.220.
131.1. *tablet*] miniature.

<blockquote>

To trifle in disputes, or vainly struggle 135
With that eternal mercy which protects us.
Come home, home to my heart, thou banished peace!
My ecstasy of joys would speak in passion
But that I would not lose that part of man
Which is reserved to entertain content. 140
Eroclea, I am thine; O, let me seize thee
As my inheritance. Hymen shall now
Set all his torches burning to give light
Throughout this land, new-settled in thy welcome.

Eroclea. You are still gracious. Sir, how I have lived, 145
By what means been conveyed, by what preserved,
By what returned, Rhetias, my trusty servant,
Directed by the wisdom of my uncle,
The good Sophronos, can inform at large.

Palador. Enough. Instead of music, every night, 150
To make our sleeps delightful, thou shalt close
Our weary eyes with some part of thy story.

Eroclea. O, but my father!

Palador.   Fear not; to behold
Eroclea safe will make him young again;
It shall be our first task. Blush, sensual follies, 155
Which are not guarded with thoughts chastely pure.
There is no faith in lust, but baits of arts;
'Tis virtuous love keeps clear contracted hearts.
                              [*Exeunt.*]

</blockquote>

137. banished peace] *banisht-peace* Q.   158.1. *Exeunt*] *Weber.*

139–40. *that . . . content*] i.e. the reason.

142–3. *Hymen . . . burning*] The god of marriage was represented as carrying a torch and veil.

145. *still*] always.

157. *baits of arts*] crafty enticements.

157–8.] Each of these lines begins with double inverted commas in Q to indicate a *sententia*.

Act V

ACT V SCENE i

Enter CORAX *and* CLEOPHILA.

Corax. 'Tis well, 'tis well; the hour is at hand
Which must conclude the business that no art
Could all this while make ripe for wished content.
O, lady, in the turmoils of our lives
Men are like politic states, or troubled seas, 5
Tossed up and down with several storms and tempests,
Change and variety of wracks and fortunes,
Till, labouring to the havens of our homes,
We struggle for the calm that crowns our ends.
Cleophila. A happy end heaven bless us with!
Corax. 'Tis well said. 10
The old man sleeps still soundly.
Cleophila. May soft dreams
Play in his fancy that, when he awakes,
With comfort he may, by degrees, digest
The present blessings in a moderate joy.
Corax. I drenched his cup to purpose; he ne'er stirred 15
At barber or at tailor; 'a will laugh
At his own metamorphosis, and wonder.
We must be watchful. Does the coach stand ready?

Act V] Actus V. Scena I. *Q.*   18. coach] *Q;* couch *Weber.*

---

1. *hour*] dissyllabic.
15. *drenched*] drugged.
18. *coach*] Other editors emend to 'couch' but Q's reading here is uniform with Q's 'coach' (V.i.178) and '*in a coach*' (V.ii.0.1.); see Introduction, pp. 38–9. Since stage chariots were used in masques and plays, Elizabethan public theatre plays such as Marlowe's *Tamburlaine*, Lodge's *Wounds of Civil War*, Dekker's *Phaeton* (the play is lost but its chariot is recorded in Henslowe's Diary in an inventory of stage properties for 10 March 1598) and a late

SC I] THE LOVER'S MELANCHOLY 135

Cleophila. All as you commanded.

      Enter TROLLIO.

         What's your haste for?
Trollio. A brace of big women, ushered by the young old ape   20
 with his she-clog at his bum, are entered the castle. Shall
 they come on?
Corax. By any means; the time is precious now.
 Lady, be quick and careful. Follow, Trollio.
Trollio. I owe all sir-reverence to your right worshipfulness.   25
       [*Exeunt* CORAX *and* TROLLIO.]
Cleophila. So many fears, so many joys encounter
 My doubtful expectations, that I waver
 Between the resolution of my hopes
 And my obedience. 'Tis not—O my fate!—
 The apprehension of a timely blessing   30
 In pleasures shakes my weakness, but the danger
 Of a mistaken duty that confines
 The limits of my reason. Let me live,
 Virtue, to thee as chaste as truth to time!

      Enter THAMASTA.

Thamasta. Attend me till I call——My sweet Cleophila!   35
Cleophila. Great princess——
Thamasta.   I bring peace, to sue a pardon
 For my neglect of all those noble virtues
 Thy mind and duty are apparelled with.
 I have deserved ill from thee, and must say

19.1.] *Dyce; after l. 18 Q.*   25.1 *Exeunt* CORAX *and* TROLLIO] *This ed.; separate exits at ll. 24, 25 Gifford.*

Blackfriars play, *The Bashful Lover* (1636) by Massinger, there is no *a priori* reason to reject 'coach'. The entry of Meleander in a coach, drawn on or discovered by pulling back a curtain, is consistent with his final honoured status.
 20. *brace . . . women*] i.e. Thamasta and Eroclea; 'big': noble, important.
 20–1. *young . . . she-clog*] i.e. Cuculus and Grilla.
 28. *resolution of*] answer to.
 29. *obedience*] i.e. to her father.
 29–33. *'Tis . . . reason*] The 'timely blessing' is her anticipated marriage, and her 'mistaken duty' is the care of her father about which she may be mistakenly conscientious; it is uncertainty about the latter which inhibits decisive thought.

  Thou art too gentle if thou canst forget it.   40
Cleophila. Alas, you have not wronged me; for, indeed,
 Acquaintance with my sorrows and my fortune
 Were grown to such familiarity,
 That 'twas an impudence more than presumption
 To wish so great a lady as you are   45
 Should lose affection on my uncle's son;
 But that your brother, equal in your blood,
 Should stoop to such a lowness as to love
 A castaway, a poor despisèd maid,
 Only for me to hope was almost sin;   50
 Yet, troth, I never tempted him.
Thamasta.   Chide not
 The grossness of my trespass, lovely sweetness,
 In such an humble language; I have smarted
 Already in the wounds my pride hath made
 Upon thy sufferings. Henceforth 'tis in you   55
 To work my happiness.
Cleophila.   Call any service
 Of mine a debt, for such it is; the letter
 You lately sent me, in the blest contents
 It made me privy to, hath largely quitted
 Every suspicion of your grace or goodness.   60
Thamasta. Let me embrace thee with a sister's love,
 A sister's love, Cleophila; for should
 My brother henceforth study to forget
 The vows that he hath made thee, I would ever
 Solicit thy deserts.
Amethus. ⎱
Menaphon. ⎰ [*Within.*] We must have entrance!   65
Thamasta. Must? Who are they, say must? You are
 unmannerly.

     Enter AMETHUS *and* MENAPHON.

 Brother, is't you? and you too, sir?
Amethus.   Your ladyship

65. *Within*] *So Gifford.*   66.1.] *Gifford; after* deserts *l.* 65 *Q.*

---

 47. *equal . . . blood*] equal to you in rank.
 59. *quitted*] cleared.
 65. *solicit thy deserts*] plead for what your worthiness deserves.

    Has had a time of scolding to your humour;
    Does the storm hold still?
Cleophila.   Never fell a shower
    More seasonably gentle on the barren   70
    Parched thirsty earth, than showers of courtesy
    Have from this princess been distilled on me,
    To make my growth in quiet of my mind
    Secure and lasting.
Thamasta.   You may both believe
    That I was not uncivil.
Amethus.   Pish! I know   75
    Her spirit and her envy.
Cleophila.   Now, in troth, sir—
    Pray credit me, I do not use to swear—
    The virtuous princess hath in words and carriage
    Been kind, so over-kind, that I do blush
    I am not rich enough in thanks sufficient   80
    For her unequalled bounty——My good cousin
    I have a suit to you.
Menaphon.   It shall be granted.
Cleophila. That no time, no persuasion, no respects
    Of jealousies past, present, or hereafter
    By possibility to be conceived,   85
    Draw you from that sincerity and pureness
    Of love which you have oftentimes protested
    To this great worthy lady; she deserves
    A duty more than what the ties of marriage
    Can claim or warrant. Be for ever hers,   90
    As she is yours, and heaven increase your comforts!
Amethus. Cleophila hath played the churchman's part;
    I'll not forbid the banns.
Menaphon.   Are you consented?
Thamasta. I have one task in charge first which concerns me:
    Brother, be not more cruel than this lady;   95
    She hath forgiven my follies, so may you.
    Her youth, her beauty, innocence, discretion,
    Without additions of estate or birth,
    Are dower for a prince indeed. You loved her,
    For sure you swore you did; else, if you did not,   100
    Here fix your heart and thus resolve: if now

79. blush] *Dyce;* blush: *Q.*

>   You miss this heaven on earth you cannot find
>   In any other choice ought but a hell.
> *Amethus.* The ladies are turned lawyers and plead
>   handsomely
>   Their clients' cases. I am an easy judge,   105
>   And so shalt thou be, Menaphon. I give thee
>   My sister for a wife; a good one, friend.
> *Menaphon.* Lady, will you confirm the gift?
> *Thamasta.*   The errors
>   Of my mistaken judgement being lost
>   To your remembrance, I shall ever strive   110
>   In my obedience to deserve your pity.
> *Menaphon.* My love, my care, my all!
> *Amethus.*   What rests for me?
>   I'm still a bachelor. Sweet maid, resolve me:
>   May I yet call you mine?
> *Cleophila.*   My Lord Amethus,
>   Blame not my plainness; I am young and simple,   115
>   And have not any power to dispose
>   Mine own will without warrant from my father;
>   That purchased, I am yours.
> *Amethus.*   It shall suffice me.

Enter CUCULUS, PELIAS, TROLLIO, *and* GRILLA
plucked in by 'em.

> *Cuculus.* Revenge! I must have revenge; I will have revenge,
>   bitter and abominable revenge; I will have revenge. This 120
>   unfashionable mongrel, this linsey-woolsey of
>   mortality—by this hand, mistress—this she-rogue is
>   drunk, and clapper-clawed me without any reverence to
>   my person or good garments. Why d'ee not speak,
>   gentlemen?   125
> *Pelias.* Some certain blows have passed, and't like your
>   highness.
> *Trollio.* Some few knocks of friendship, some love-toys, some
>   cuffs in kindness, or so.
> *Grilla.* I'll turn him away; he shall be my master no longer.

---

121. *linsey-woolsey*] strange medley; linsey-woolsey was woven from a mixture of flax and wool. In the drama of the period it is always spoken of contemptuously (Linthicum, p. 81).
123. *clapper-clawed*] thrashed.

SC I] THE LOVER'S MELANCHOLY 139

Menaphon. Is this your she-page, Cuculus? 'Tis a boy, sure. 130
Cuculus. A boy, an arrant boy in long coats.
Trollio. He has mumbled his nose, that 'tis as big as a great
    codpiece.
Cuculus. O, thou cock-vermin of iniquity!
Thamasta. Pelias, take hence the wag and school him for't. 135
    For your part, servant, I'll entreat the prince
    To grant you some fit place about his wardrobe.
Cuculus. Ever after a bloody nose do I dream of good luck. I
    horribly thank your ladyship.
    Whilst I'm in office, the old garb shall again 140
    Grow in request, and tailors shall be men.
    Come, Trollio, help to wash my face, prithee.
Trollio. Yes, and to scour it too.
        Exeunt CUCULUS, TROLLIO, PELIAS, GRILL[A].

        Enter RHETIAS, CORAX.

Rhetias. The prince and princess are at hand; give over
    Your amorous dialogues. Most honoured lady, 145
    Henceforth forbear your sadness; are you ready
    To practise your instructions?
Cleophila.   I have studied
    My part with care, and will perform it, Rhetias,
    With all the skill I can.
Corax.   I'll pass my word for her.

    Flourish. Enter PALADOR, SOPHRONOS, ARETUS, *and* EROCLEA.

Palador. Thus princes should be circled, with a guard 150
    Of truly noble friends and watchful subjects.
    O, Rhetias, thou art just; the youth thou told'st me
    That lived at Athens, is returned at last
    To her own fortunes and contracted love.
Rhetias. My knowledge made me sure of my report, sir. 155
Palador. Eroclea, clear thy fears; when the sun shines
    Clouds must not dare to muster in the sky

143. too.] too.——Q. 143.1. *Exeunt*] *Gifford; Exit* Q. 144–7.] *Weber; prose in* Q. 149.1. PALADOR] *Prince* Q.

---

  132. *mumbled*] mauled.
  135. *school*] discipline.
  140–1. *old . . . request*] the former custom (of having male pages) shall again become fashionable.

Nor shall they here——Why do they kneel? Stand up,
The day and place is privileged.
Sophronos. Your presence,
Great sir, makes every room a sanctuary.   160
Palador. Wherefore does this young virgin use such
   circumstance
In duty to us? Rise.
Eroclea. 'Tis I must raise her.
Forgive me, sister; I have been too private
In hiding from your knowledge any secret
That should have been in common 'twixt our souls;   165
But I was ruled by counsel.
Cleophila. That I show
Myself a girl, sister, and bewray
Joy in too soft a passion 'fore all these,
I hope you cannot blame me.   [*They weep and embrace.*]
Palador. We must part
The sudden meeting of these two fair rivulets   170
With th'island of our arms. Cleophila,
The custom of thy piety hath built,
Even to thy younger years, a monument
Of memorable fame; some great reward
Must wait on thy desert.
Sophronos. The prince speaks t'ee, niece.   175
Corax. Chat low, I pray; let's about our business.
The good old man awakes. My lord, withdraw.
Rhetias, let's settle here the coach.
Palador. Away then!
            Exeunt.

---

169. *They weep and embrace*] *Weeps, and falls into the arms of Ero.* Gifford.   178. coach] *Q;* couch Weber.   178.1. *Exeunt*] Gifford; *Exeunt all, except* RHETIAS, CORAX, *and a Boy* Weber; *Exit Q.*

---

159. *privileged*] exempt from the customary forms of ceremony.
160. *sanctuary*] the most sacred part of a church; hence the kneeling.
167. *bewray*] reveal.
169–71. *We ... arms*] The metaphor for parting Eroclea and Cleophila is more pretty than exact.
178. *coach*] On this and the stage direction at the beginning of the next scene see note to V.i.18.

Act V Scene ii

Soft music. Enter MELEANDER *in a coach, his hair and beard trimmed, habit and gown changed.* RHETIAS *and* CORAX, *and* Boy *that sings.*

The Song.

Fly hence, shadows, that do keep
    Watchful sorrows charmed in sleep!
Though the eyes be overtaken,
    Yet the heart doth ever waken
Thoughts chained up in busy snares   5
    Of continual woes and cares;
Love and griefs are so expressed
    As they rather sigh than rest.
Fly hence, shadows, that do keep
    Watchful sorrows charmed in sleep!   10

Meleander. [*Awakening.*] Where am I? Ha! What sounds are these? 'Tis day, sure.
    O, I have slept belike; 'tis but the foolery
Of some beguiling dream. So, so! I will not
Trouble the play of my delighted fancy,
But dream my dream out.
Corax.   Morrow to your lordship!   15
    You took a jolly nap, and slept it soundly.
Meleander. Away beast! Let me alone.
Corax.   O, by your leave, sir,
I must be bold to raise ye, else your physic
Will turn to further sickness.
Meleander.   Physic, bear-leech?
Corax. Yes, physic; you are mad.   20
Meleander. Trollio! Cleophila!
Rhetias.   Sir, I am here.
Meleander. I know thee, Rhetias; prithee rid the room

Scene division this ed. 0.1. *in a coach*] Q; *on a Couch* Weber. 1–10.] *Italics in* Q *except* eyes *l.*3, heart *l.* 4. 11. *Awakening*] *So* Gifford.

    1–10.] A seventeenth-century musical setting of this song is given in Appendix B.
    16. *jolly*] fine.
    19. *bear-leech*] Cf. note to IV.ii.3.

Of this tormenting noise. *Cease music.* He tells me, sirrah,
I have took physic, Rhetias; physic, physic!
Rhetias. Sir, true, you have; and this most learnèd scholar
Applied 't 'ee. O, you were in dangerous plight
Before he took ye in hand.
Meleander. These things are drunk,
Directly drunk. Where did you get your liquor?
Corax. I never saw a body in the wane
Of age so overspread with several sorts
Of such diseases as the strength of youth
Would groan under and sink.
Rhetias. The more your glory
In the miraculous cure.
Corax. Bring me the cordial
Prepared for him to take after his sleep;
'Twill do him good at heart.
Rhetias. I hope it will, sir. *Exit.*
Meleander. What dost think I am, that thou shouldst fiddle
So much upon my patience? Fool, the weight
Of my disease sits on my heart so heavy
That all the hands of art cannot remove
One grain to ease my grief. If thou couldst poison
My memory, or wrap my senses up
Into a dulness hard and cold as flints;
If thou couldst make me walk, speak, eat, and laugh,
Without a sense or knowledge of my faculties,
Why, then, perhaps, at marts thou mightst make benefit
Of such an antic motion, and get credit
From credulous gazers, but not profit me.
Study to gull the wise; I am too simple
To be wrought on.
Corax. I'll burn my books, old man,

23. *Cease music*] *This ed.; after* alone *l. 17 Q.* 26. Applied't 'ee] Applied't ye *Dyce;* Apply'd t'ee *Q.* 27. in hand] *Weber;* hand *Q.*

---

23. *noise*] often used of music and without the frequent modern connotation of harshness.
28. *Directly*] plainly.
36. *fiddle*] play idly.
45–6. *at . . . motion*] at fairs you might make some profit out of such a grotesque puppet show.
47. *credulous gazers*] i.e. believing Meleander to be a puppet.

SC II]   THE LOVER'S MELANCHOLY   143

 But I will do thee good, and quickly too. 50

   Enter ARETUS *with a patent.*

Aretus. Most honoured Lord Meleander, our great master,
 Prince Palador of Cyprus, hath by me
 Sent you this patent, in which is contained
 Not only confirmation of the honours
 You formerly enjoyed, but the addition 55
 Of the marshalship of Cyprus; and ere long
 He means to visit you. Excuse my haste,
 I must attend the prince. *Exit.*
Corax.   There's one pill works.
Meleander. Dost know that spirit? 'Tis a grave familiar,
 And talked I know not what.
Corax.   He's like, methinks, 60
 The prince his tutor, Aretus.
Meleander.   Yes, yes;
 It may be I have seen such a formality;
 No matter where or when.

   Enter AMETHUS *with a staff.*

Amethus.   The prince hath sent ye,
 My lord, this staff of office, and withal
 Salutes you Grand Commander of the Ports 65
 Throughout his principalities. He shortly
 Will visit you himself. I must attend him. *Exit.*
Corax. D'ee feel your physic stirring yet?
Meleander.   A devil
 Is a rare juggler, and can cheat the eye
 But not corrupt the reason in the throne 70

58. prince.] Prince.——*Q.* 67. him.] him.——*Q.*

 50.1ff.] This arresting device of a sequence of messengers is also used in the denouement of *The Broken Heart*, V.ii.12ff. (ed. T. J. B. Spencer, London, 1980).
 53. *patent*] letters patent granting some privilege or office.
 59. *familiar*] demon, supposedly associated with or controlled by a man or woman; witches had their familiars as we find in *The Witch of Edmonton*, a play in which Ford collaborated.
 62. *formality*] ceremonious person; *O.E.D.* does not record this usage.
 68–71. *A devil . . . soul*] Cf. IV.iii.22–4 and note.

144   THE LOVER'S MELANCHOLY   [ACT V

  Of a pure soul.

     Enter SOPHRONOS *with a tablet.*

       ——Another? I will stand thee,
  Be what thou canst, I care not.
Sophronos.   From the prince,
  Dear brother, I present you this rich relic,
  A jewel he hath long worn in his bosom.
  Henceforth, he bade me say, he does beseech you   75
  To call him son, for he will call you father.
  It is an honour, brother, that a subject
  Cannot but entertain with thankful prayers.
  Be moderate in your joys; he will in person
  Confirm my errand, but commands my service.   *Exit.*   80
Corax. What hope now of your cure?
Meleander.   Stay, stay!——What earthquakes
  Roll in my flesh? Here's prince, and prince, and prince,
  Prince upon prince! The dotage of my sorrows
  Revels in magic of ambitious scorn.
  Be they enchantments deadly as the grave   85
  I'll look upon 'em; patent, staff, and relic.
  To the last first. [*Taking up the miniature.*] Round me, ye
    guarding ministers,
  And ever keep me waking till the cliffs
  That overhang my sight fall off, and leave
  These hollow spaces to be crammed with dust!   90
Corax. 'Tis time, I see, to fetch the cordial. Prithee,
  Sit down; I'll instantly be here again.   *Exit.*
Meleander. Good, give me leave, I will sit down indeed;
  Here's company enough for me to prate to.
  Eroclea! 'Tis the same; the cunning artsman   95
  Faltered not in a line. Could he have fashioned
  A little hollow space here, and blown breath
  To have made it move and whisper, 't had been excellent.

71.1.] *Weber; after* care not *l.* 72 *Q.*   87. *Taking up the miniature*] *So Gifford.*   92. again.] againe——*Q.*

  71.1. tablet] miniature of Eroclea referred to at IV.iii.130.
  71. *Another*] another familiar.
  stand] withstand.
  84. *magic . . . scorn*] mocking delusions of grandeur.
  88. *cliffs*] eyebrows and/or eyelids; a strained and grotesque metaphor.

But, faith, 'tis well, 'tis very well as 'tis;
Passing, most passing well.

Enter CLEOPHILA, EROCLEA, RHETIAS.

Cleophila.   The sovereign greatness,   100
Who by commission from the powers of heaven
Sways both this land and us, our gracious prince,
By me presents you, sir, with this large bounty,
A gift more precious to him than his birthright.
Here let your cares take end; now set at liberty   105
Your long-imprisoned heart, and welcome home
The solace of your soul, too long kept from you.
Eroclea. [*Kneeling.*] Dear sir, you know me?
Meleander.   Yes, thou art my daughter,
My eldest blessing. Know thee? Why, Eroclea,
I never did forget thee in thy absence.   110
Poor soul, how dost?
Eroclea.   The best of my well-being
Consists in yours.
Meleander.   Stand up; the gods, who hitherto
Have kept us both alive, preserve thee ever!
Cleophila, I thank thee and the prince.
I thank thee too, Eroclea, that thou wouldst,   115
In pity of my age, take so much pains
To live till I might once more look upon thee
Before I broke my heart. O, 'twas a piece
Of piety and duty unexampled!
Rhetias. [*Aside.*] The good man relisheth his comforts
    strangely;   120
The sight doth turn me child.
Eroclea.   I have not words
That can express my joys.
Cleophila.   Nor I.
Meleander.   Nor I.
Yet let us gaze on one another freely
And surfeit with our eyes. Let me be plain:
If I should speak as much as I should speak,   125
I should talk of a thousand things at once,
And all of thee, of thee, my child, of thee!

108. *Kneeling*] *So Gifford.*   120. *Aside*] *Gifford.*

---

  121. *doth . . . child*] makes me weep.

My tears, like ruffling winds locked up in caves,
Do bustle for a vent——On t'other side,
To fly out into mirth were not so comely.
Come hither, let me kiss thee——With a pride,
Strength, courage, and fresh blood, which now thy
    presence
Hath stored me with, I kneel before their altars
Whose sovereignty kept guard about thy safety.
Ask, ask thy sister, prithee, she'll tell thee
How I have been much mad.
Cleophila.   Much discontented,
Shunning all means that might procure him comfort.
Eroclea. Heaven has at last been gracious.
Meleander.   So say I;
But wherefore drop thy words in such a sloth
As if thou wert afraid to mingle truth
With thy misfortunes? Understand me throughly:
I would not have thee to report at large,
From point to point, a journal of thy absence,
'Twill take up too much time; I would securely
Engross the little remnant of my life
That thou mightst every day be telling somewhat
Which might convey me to my rest with comfort.
Let me bethink me; how we parted first
Puzzles my faint remembrance——But soft,
Cleophila, thou toldst me that the prince
Sent me this present.
Cleophila.   From his own fair hands
I did receive my sister.
Meleander.   To requite him,
We will not dig his father's grave anew,
Although the mention of him much concerns
The business we inquire of——As I said,
We parted in a hurry at the court,
I to this castle, after made my jail;
But whither thou, dear heart?
Rhetias.   Now they fall to't;

---
148. me; how . . . first] *So Weber;* me, how . . . first: *Q.*

140–1. mingle . . . misfortunes] tell the truth about your misfortunes.
145.] either 'grant the rest of my life the monopoly' (of your story), or 'entirely occupy the rest of my life'.

   I looked for this.
Eroclea.   I, by my uncle's care,
 Sophronos, my good uncle, suddenly   160
 Was like a sailor's boy conveyed a-shipboard
 That very night.
Meleander.   A policy quick and strange.
Eroclea. The ship was bound for Corinth; whither first,
 Attended only with your servant, Rhetias,
 And all fit necessaries, we arrived;   165
 From thence, in habit of a youth, we journeyed
 To Athens, where till our return of late
 Have we lived safe.
Meleander.   O, what a thing is man
 To bandy factions of distempered passions
 Against the sacred providence above him!   170
 Here, in the legend of thy two years' exile,
 Rare pity and delight are sweetly mixed.
 And still thou wert a boy?
Eroclea.   So I obeyed
 My uncle's wise command.
Meleander.   'Twas safely carried,
 I humbly thank thy fate.
Eroclea.   If earthly treasures 175
 Are poured in plenty down from heaven on mortals,
 They reign amongst those oracles that flow
 In schools of sacred knowledge; such is Athens.
 Yet Athens was to me but a fair prison;
 The thoughts of you, my sister, country, fortunes, 180
 And something of the prince, barred all contents
 Which else might ravish sense. For had not Rhetias
 Been always comfortable to me, certainly
 Things had gone worse.
Meleander.   Speak low, Eroclea;

159–62.] *Weber; prose in* Q. 177. reign] *Q;* rain *Dyce.*

 162. *quick*] acute.
 169. *bandy*] make a confederacy of.
 171. *legend*] story, account.
 177. *reign*] Q reigne. Dyce emends to 'rain' and although this agrees with the metaphors 'poured' and 'flow' there is no good reason to suspect Q's 'reigne' which makes satisfactory sense.
 183. *comfortable*] supporting and encouraging.

That 'something of the prince' bears danger in it. 185
Yet thou hast travelled, wench, for such endowments
As might create a prince a wife fit for him
Had he the world to guide; but touch not there.
How cam'st thou home?

Rhetias.   Sir, with your noble favour,
Kissing your hand first, that point I can answer. 190

Meleander. Honest, right honest Rhetias.

Rhetias.   Your grave brother
Perceived with what a hopeless love his son,
Lord Menaphon, too eagerly pursued
Thamasta, cousin to our present prince;
And to remove the violence of affection 195
Sent him to Athens, where for twelve months space
Your daughter, my young lady, and her cousin
Enjoyed each other's griefs; till by his father,
The Lord Sophronos, we were all called home.

Meleander. Enough, enough; the world shall henceforth witness 200
My thankfulness to heaven and those people
Who have been pitiful to me and mine.
Lend me a looking-glass——How now! How came I
So courtly in fresh raiments?

Rhetias.   Here's the glass, sir.

Meleander. [*Looking in the mirror.*] I'm in the trim too——O
Cleophila, 205
This was the goodness of thy care and cunning——
            Loud music.
Whence comes this noise?

Rhetias.   The prince, my lord, in person.

Enter PALADOR, SOPHRONOS, ARETUS, MENAPHON,
THAMASTA, CORAX, KALA.

Palador. Ye shall not kneel to us; rise all, I charge ye.
Father, you wrong your age; henceforth my arms

---

205. *Looking in the mirror*] *This ed.*   207.1. PALADOR] *Prince Q.*

186. *travelled*] Q *trauayl'd*. Ford could have intended either 'travailed' or 'travelled'; Eroclea had travelled to Athens and had apparently also travailed (studied) at the 'schools of sacred knowledge' (V.ii.178).
198. *Enjoyed . . . griefs*] took solace in the exchange of griefs.
205. *in the trim*] He was barbered while asleep.

    And heart shall be your guard. We have o'erheard 210
    All passages of your united loves;
    Be young again, Meleander; live to number
    A happy generation and die old
    In comforts as in years! The offices
    And honours which I late on thee conferred 215
    Are not fantastic bounties but thy merit;
    Enjoy them liberally.
Meleander.   My tears must thank ye
    For my tongue cannot.
Corax.   I have kept my promise
    And given you a sure cordial.
Meleander.   O, a rare one!
Palador. Good man, we both have shared enough of sadness, 220
    Though thine has tasted deeper of th'extreme;
    Let us forget it henceforth. Where's the picture
    I sent ye? Keep it, 'tis a counterfeit;
    And in exchange of that I seize on this,
    The real substance. With this other hand 225
    I give away before her father's face
    His younger joy, Cleophila, to thee,
    Cousin Amethus; take her, and be to her
    More than a father, a deserving husband.
    Thus robbed of both thy children in a minute, 230
    Thy cares are taken off.
Meleander.   My brains are dulled;
    I am entranced and know not what you mean.
    Great, gracious sir, alas, why do you mock me?
    I am a weak old man, so poor and feeble
    That my untoward joints can scarcely creep 235
    Unto the grave where I must seek my rest.
Palador. Eroclea was, you know, contracted mine;
    Cleophila my cousin's, by consent
    Of both their hearts; we both now claim our own.
    It only rests in you to give a blessing 240
    For confirmation.

---

  213. *generation*] offspring, i.e. grandchildren.
  232. *entranced*] either 'in a trance', or 'overpowered with strength of feeling' (*O.E.D.*, vb.2).
  235. *untoward*] clumsy.
  237–9.] On the difference between two the betrothals see note to II.i.162–6.

Rhetias. Sir, 'tis truth and justice.
Meleander. The gods that lent ye to me, bless your vows!
O children, children, pay your prayers to heaven
For they have showed much mercy. But, Sophronos,
Thou art my brother—I can say no more— 245
A good, good brother!
Palador. Leave the rest to time.
Cousin Thamasta, I must give you too.
She's thy wife, Menaphon. Rhetias, for thee
And Corax, I have more than common thanks.
On to the temple! There all solemn rites 250
Performed, a general feast shall be proclaimed.
The Lover's Melancholy hath found cure;
Sorrows are changed to bride-songs. So they thrive
Whom fate, in spite of storms, hath kept alive.
Exeunt omnes.

FINIS.

243–4. *heaven . . . they*] Singular 'heaven' with plural concord is paralleled in Shakespeare; e.g. *R2*, I.ii.6–7.

EPILOGUE

To be too confident is as unjust
In any work as too much to distrust;
Who from the laws of study have not swerved
Know begged applauses never were deserved.
We must submit to censure; so doth he 5
Whose hours begot this issue; yet, being free,
For his part, if he have not pleased you, then
In this kind he'll not trouble you again.

FINIS.

---

5. *censure*] judgement.
6. *free*] Two senses are probably combined here: 'under no obligation to you' and 'not obliged to write for a living', the latter connecting with the gentleman-amateur's scornful remark in the Prologue about those who make a trade of poetry (l. 12).

APPENDIX A
Source of the 'Musical Duel': I.i.106–70

Famiamus Strada, *Prolusiones Academicae, Oratoriae, Historicae, Poeticae* (1617): Liber 2, Prolusio 6, Academicae 2. Ford's imitation of Strada's poem is discussed in the Introduction, pp. 4–5. The following is a close translation of the florid Latin original.

> Now the sun was declining from the meridian of its round, shaking the fire more gently from its hair-like rays, when close by Tiber's flood a lutanist was beguiling his cares with his sounding lute and, sheltered by a dark oak and the verdant setting, eased the heat of the day.
>
> A nightingale, visitor from a neighbouring wood—muse of the place and harmless siren of the grove—heard him. And drawing near she remained hidden by the foliage, and taking deep impression of the sound murmured it over to herself, and the measures he varied with his fingers she gave back with her throat.
>
> The lutanist became aware of the nightingale echoing him with her imitation and resolved to make sport with the bird. And so he puts his lute to fuller proof and, offering trial of the coming contest, forthwith runs over all the strings with nimble touch. She with equal liveliness giving forth a thousand notes of varying tone displays a subtle taste of the singing to come. Then the lutanist moving his right hand through the quivering strings now, as if contemptuous, strikes them asunder with his finger and combs down the chords with measured and simple address; now he goes back over them separately and plies the strings piecemeal with flashing fingers, and re-echoes with swift stroke. Thereupon he falls silent. She replies with just so many measures and answers art with art. Now, as if in doubt of her unpolished singing, she utters a long note and enters upon a song free of intricate turns, like succeeding like, and in continuous flow gives forth from her breast a liquid passage with sinking voice. Now she changes to short phrases, melodious and brief cadences. She ponders her song, ebbs and flows with quivering utterance.
>
> The lutanist marvels at such a sweet and various song coming from that small throat and, attempting greater things, he with astonishing skill makes his lute play first this and then that; while he whirls upon the treble strings and attacks the bass, striking with powerful blows, he at the same time intermingles a harsh tumult of sound as if with the noise he were rousing up lazy soldiers to battle. The nightingale sings this also and, while with liquid voice she passionately sends forth a trembling sound and interweaves agreeable short measures, unexpectedly she rolls out a bass note and a light murmur stirs within her, brightening with one sound and darkening with the other as if she sounded trumpets of war.

APPENDIX A

The lutanist, not surprisingly, went red in the face and with burning anger says, 'Sylvan lute player, either you will not echo what I shall play now or I will withdraw my feeble lute.' Saying no more he urges on his lute to inimitable harmonies, for indeed he flies through the strings with his hand, searches out this and that measure and works at every string, hums and tinkles, swells more proudly, multiplies by repetition, and strikes in a copious dance of sound. Then he stood waiting to see if his rival would produce anything in reply. She, however, although her former arduous singing has made her throat harsh, unwilling to be defeated, at once but vainly summons up all her strength. For a while she attempts to render such and so many different notes of the lute with her artless and simple voice, and to imitate the powerful strains with her tiny pipes. Unequal to her great-souled daring and unequal to her grief she ceases, and giving up her life at the height of battle falls upon the lute of her victor, having found a fitting grave. Thus far does emulation carry delicate souls.

APPENDIX B

Musical setting of 'Fly hence, shadows, that do keep': V.ii.1–10.

This, the only known setting of the song, is by John Wilson (1595–1674). It was published in the composer's old age in his *Cheerful Ayres or Ballads* (Oxford, 1660). The title page of this collection states that the contents were 'First composed for one single Voice and since set for three Voices', presumably to render them more versatile for domestic music-making. From 1614 Wilson was connected with the King's Men, providing music for the court and London stage, and between 1622 and 1637 he was one of the 'Servants of the City for Music and voice'. It is thus likely that the present setting was made for the first performance of the play (1628).

The text published by Wilson differs from Ford's (here set to the music) in a few details, of which the following are significant:

Line no.	Ford	Wilson
5	chained	charm'd
6	woes	toyles
8	As	That

At bar 5 'in' was originally placed one note earlier. This has been altered in conformity with bar 22, and the preceding slur extended accordingly. Accidentals redundant in the light of modern notational convention are omitted, and editorial accidentals are placed above the note they affect. A skeletal realization of the thoroughbass has been provided in a range appropriate to the lute or keyboard instruments. Players of the theorbo will need to dispose much of the accompaniment in a lower range.

According to Wilson's preface (fol. 2), the 'CANTUS PRIMUS is a complete Booke of its selfe, carrying the principall Ayre to Sing alone with a through Base. CANTUS SECUNDUS and BASSUS are also printed singly [in separate partbooks] to make two, or three Parts, as shall be requisite for the Company that will use them.' Since the stage direction at the beginning of V.ii indicates that the song was sung by a boy, it is the earlier form (cantus 1 and thoroughbass) that was

APPENDIX B 155

presumably used for the original performances. The later alternatives are:

    cantus 1, cantus 2 and thoroughbass
    cantus 1 and bassus
    cantus 1, cantus 2 and bassus } with or without thoroughbass

The cantus parts might alternatively be sung an octave lower than written, by tenors. Bowed instruments (violin and viol) might play the lower parts, especially if not sung. The pitch of the accompanying instruments is likely to have been between a semitone and a tone below the modern standard.

Transcript and editorial note by Lewis Jones.

Glossarial Index to the Commentary

Words are generally cited in the form in which they appear in the text but where a word occurs in different forms the basic form only is given. An asterisk indicates information which supplements that found in *O.E.D.*

Affected, II.i.135
affections, II.i.91
allow, *Commend. Verses* by George Donne, 6
antic *sb.* I.ii.13; *adj*, I.i.74, II.i.5, V.ii.46; *adv*, III.iii.26.1
apparition, IV.iii.19
apprehension, III.ii.71
arts, IV.iii.157
avoid, *Ep. Ded.*, 18, I.ii.122

*Back door, III.i.68
balloon ball, II.i.53
ban-dog, I.ii.109
bandy *vb*, V.ii.169
barbers, I.ii.115
bare *adj*, I.ii.37
bays *sb*, *Commend. Verses* by George Donne, 4
bear-leech, V.ii.19
bedlam, II.i.65, III.iii.54.1
*bewray, V.i.167
big, III.i.7, V.i.20
blood, III.ii.126, V.i.47
botchers, I.ii.133
bounce *sb*, I.i.11, III.iii.69; *vb*, IV.ii.44
brach, I.ii.80
buckler, I.ii.31
buss *vb*, III.iii.51
butterfly, II.i.46
buzz *sb*, I.ii.22, IV.ii.77
bye *sb*, *Prologue*, 16
by possibility, IV.iii.36–7

Carmen, II.ii.113
carriage, II.i.320

cast *vb*, I.ii.114, 163
censure *sb*, *Epilogue*, 5
*centre *sb*, I.i.143
charm *vb*, II.i.174
choler, *Commend. Verses* by Humfrey Howorth, 1
cittern, II.i.39
clapper-clawed, V.i.123
clefs, I.i.135
clew *sb*, IV.ii.60
close-stool, IV.ii.2
closet *sb*, I.iii.78
cod of musk, III.i.28–9
codpieces, II.ii.18
cokes, IV.ii.181
complimentally, I.ii.41
conceit *sb*, II.i.94
*conceit *sb*, III.i.25
condition, I.ii.129
condolements, III.i.37
*conjure up a spirit, IV.ii.204
consent *sb*, IV.ii.138
contents *sb*, I.iii.52
contract *sb*, II.i.166
conundrumed, II.ii.51
convoy *sb*, IV.iii.116
course *sb*, III.iii.48
court *vb*, II.i.158
courtship, I.ii.35
coxcomb, III.iii.48.02
creature, I.i.36, II.i.230
creep to, III.ii.197
cross-gartered, III.i.2
crotchetted, II.ii.51
cue, III.i.72
cunning *sb*, I.i.141
curiosity, I.i.141

GLOSSARIAL INDEX TO COMMENTARY

*Dancer, I.ii.64
declined, III.ii.120
denier, I.ii.121
device, I.ii.155, III.i.89
directly, V.ii.28
discover, III.i.129, IV.i.30
distemper, II.i.27
distractions, I.i.183
division, I.i.125
dog-leeches, IV.ii.3
doodles sb, III.i.88
dotage, III.i.111
down sb, I.i.124
down sb, II.ii.36
drenched, V.i.15

Effeminated, Commend. Verses by Humfrey Howorth, 11
elixir, II.i.106
else, I.i.89
empirics, I.ii.113
engross, I.i.35, IV.ii.73
entertainments, III.ii.148
entranced, V.ii.232
equal adj, IV.iii.54

*False fires, IV.i.4
fame, IV.i.22
familiar sb, V.ii.59
fantastic adj/sb, IV.iii.18
fawned upon, I.i.66
feigned, I.i.99
fiddle vb, V.ii.36
firk vb, IV.ii.43
flatteries, IV.i.32
fond adj, II.i.327
footcloth, I.ii.65
footposts, II.ii.113
fopperies, I.i.74
forerunner, I.ii.26
*formality, V.ii.62
free adj, I.i.49, III.ii.116, Epilogue, 6

Gaffer, III.iii.50
garboils sb, III.i.37
gelding sb, III.ii.11
generation, V.ii.213
genius, IV.ii.174
good sb, I.i.121

*good turn, III.ii.51
goody, III.i.85
goodyear, II.ii.20
gratulate, I.i.2
green-sickness-livered, III.ii.17
*greatness, IV.iii.82
guarded adj, I.ii.27

Head-piece, I.ii.69, II.i.37
hood, I.ii.65
hug vb, I.ii.14
humorous, III.iii.7

Idle adj, III.ii.123
ill-humours, I.ii.140
implement sb, II.ii.33
imposterous, I.ii.132
*in metal, IV.ii.44
innocent sb, I.ii.75, I.iii.34
intelligence sb, I.ii.22
intermured, I.i.62
in the trim, V.ii.205
invention, III.iii.93

Jades sb, II.ii.116
jealous, IV.i.11
jealousy, Commend. Verses by Humfrey Howorth, 14
jolly adj, V.ii.16

Kindly, I.iii.23
know, III.ii.103

Lackeys, vb, I.ii.33
learn, II.i.307
legend, V.ii.171
linsey-woolsey, V.i.121
lost security, II.i.3

Make one, I.ii.158
May-game, I.ii.10
merchant sb, II.i.195
mineralists, I.ii.113
*model sb, IV.ii.137
moods, I.i.135
moon-calves, I.ii.98
motion sb, I.i.82, V.ii.46
mountebanks, I.ii.113
muff, I.ii.65
mumbled, V.i.132

GLOSSARIAL INDEX TO COMMENTARY 159

murrion, IV.ii.29.1
mushrooms *sb*, I.ii.8

Naught, III.ii.207
neat *adj*, I.iii.46
nectar, IV.ii.175
no boot, II.ii.27
noise *sb*, V.ii.23
nuncle, III.iii.51

Of proof, II.i.156
of the trim, I.iii.2, III.i.1
of worship, IV.ii.42
*on conscience, II.ii.13
ouzel, II.i.244

Paid in mine own coin, IV.i.78
*paper-plot, III.iii.02
pashing, I.i.161
passing over, I.ii.101.1
patent *sb*, I.ii.53, II.i.114, V.ii.53
pension *sb*, IV.i.51
*Periwinkle, I.ii.97
perstreperous, II.i.43
pieced, I.i.40
piece up, IV.ii.122
poet-apes, *Commend. Verses* by William Singleton, 13
politic, II.i.228
portly, I.iii.30
practice, I.ii.106
presence, II.i.45
pretend, II.i.73
printed, III.ii.169
privileged, V.i.159
process *sb*, I.iii.76
profession, IV.ii.151
proper, III.iii.103
puff *vb*, II.i.44
punctual, IV.ii.68

*Quab, III.iii.5
quit, *Prologue*, 13, V.i.59
quacksalvers, I.ii.113
qualify, IV.ii.16
quick *adj*, V.ii.162
quill *sb*, *Commend. Verses* by George Donne, 4
quiristers, I.i.118

Rage *sb*, *Commend. Verses* by Humfrey Howorth, 7
range *vb*, II.i.270
rape *sb*, II.i.174
rare, I.i.183
relish *sb*, II.i.185; *vb*, I.iii.76
renowns *vb*, I.ii.7
report *sb*, II.i.60, IV.i.30
*Reprieve *sb*, *Commend. Verses* by William Singleton, 9
resolution, V.i.28
resolve *vb*, I.i.111, II.i.274
respect *vb*, II.i.326
*respectively, II.ii.127
revel *vb*, II.ii.124
riotous, I.i.178
roaring *sb*, III.i.71
round *vb*, III.ii.85
running in a blood, IV.i.15

Sadness, I.iii.42, III.iii.12
satire, IV.i.32
secure *adj*, II.i.230
servant, I.iii.62, III.ii.187, IV.i.27
set me forth, I.iii.59
set of faces, III.ii.56
several *adj*, I.i.84, I.i.123, III.ii.78
'sfoot, III.i.71
shadow *sb*, III.iii.96
shag *adj*, III.iii.19.1
shame *sb*, I.iii.81
shough, III.iii.51
shrewd, III.ii.52
simples, IV.ii.77
singular, III.iii.8
slovenry, I.ii.106
soop, III.iii.60
soothe, II.i.248
sort *vb*, II.i.261
spleen, II.ii.37
squall *sb*, II.i.120
square *adj*, IV.ii.72
square out, II.i.109
stand *vb*, V.ii.71
stand on points, III.ii.8
stands at livery, III.i.8
still *adv*, IV.iii.145
stomach *sb*, II.ii.23
straggler, III.ii.37
strain, *sb*, I.i.123

*strong lines, III.i.63–4
study *vb*, II.i.288
sullen, II.ii.4
suppositors, I.ii.115

Tablet, II.i.220, V.ii.71.1
tenters, I.i.17
thing, *Commend. Verses* by
    Humfrey Howorth, 2, III.i.77
toss-pot, IV.ii.169
*trangdido, IV.ii.43
trencher, I.ii.31
Trojan, IV.ii.168
trumperies, III.i.85

Uncouth, IV.ii.51
*understanding, I.ii.71
*unity, IV.iii.46

untoward, IV.ii.29, V.ii.235

Vapours, *vb*, IV.ii.45
venture *vb*, III.ii.176
vizard, IV.iii.111
voluntaries, I.i.140

Wake *vb*, IV.ii.118
wheel about, I.ii.105
whimsied, II.ii.51
Whisk *sb*, III.i.85
widgeon, IV.ii.182
wildfire, IV.ii.100
wit *sb*, I.ii.12
with a witness, IV.ii.205
woman-surgeon, I.ii.89
woo, I.i.174
woodcock, II.i.38